LORDS OF WINTER

*AND OF LOVE*

# Lords of Winter

## *and of Love*

A BOOK OF CANADIAN LOVE POEMS
IN ENGLISH AND FRENCH

Edited with an introduction by
BARRY CALLAGHAN

Exile Editions Ltd.
TORONTO 1983

*Cover watercolor:* MICHAEL CALLAGHAN
*Drawing:* CLAIRE WEISSMAN WILKS
*Design:* HAROLD KURSCHENSKA

This edition is published by Exile Editions Limited, 69 Sullivan Street, Toronto, Canada. The publisher wishes to acknowledge the Canada Council and the Ontario Arts Council for financial assistance towards publication.

Exile Editions are distributed in Canada and the United States by Firefly Books, 3520 Pharmacy Avenue, Unit 1C, Scarborough, Ontario M1W 2T8

The title, LORDS OF WINTER AND OF LOVE, is taken from *How Weeps the Hangman*, a poem by Gwendolyn MacEwen

ISBN 0-920428-53-3

# CONTENTS

*vi*

# Introduction

W E ENDURE THE WINTER, but not in discontent. We are sometimes sapped by the long summer and are too at ease with autumn, mais, c'est la fin, c'est la fenaison. The leap of the heart is always there. Sometimes, because snow-light can become snow-blindness, we forget that frozen apples on the bough are bells, but by and large we see with clarity, the light that casts sharp shadows. We take on death directly, with delicacy and laughter, as all great lovers do. There is no love without les petits morts. Survival is a small idea, contrary to any notion of love. We are lovers whether we like it or not: ironic, with one foot in the grave, incubating in the gloom, but with visions of planets rotating around a room; or sardonic, believing God loves us like earthworms love wood and catfish love the cut-glass glory of clear water. There is nothing sadder than those who say God is dead, God being our creation of our best sense of ourselves, forgotten and then discovered coursing within us, released from snow. As lovers, crucified and reborn in our sacks of flesh, we pursue the sacred, are transformed in ancient gardens, in silent rooms, ancestral tombs: "The thought of him turns me to water ... the thought of him has made me marble." Grace and immortality.

Of course, whether we are mystical, stealing music from the moon, or wart hogs thrusting through darkness in search of the muse, or moved by the figure of a lone man actually mounting his horse, we keep a poker face. We cultivate the poker face, the wry dry tone that masks our laughter. But we are full of laughter and experiment and play. Even in our mad moments, staring at the sphinx along railroad tracks of Toronto or trapped inside the hallowe'en head of terror, we put down roots, the root, and reach for joy, holiness, celebration, the "applaudisements and bravos bombinating along the Boulevard." Though we are sometimes macho or deprecating about things that go "BOING" in the night, we are never dull. Whether in little narratives or surrealistic splinters of insight, we play, play with words and each other in two languages, siamese twins pretending the other is not there – a "presence" always "absent" in our affairs. We have the blessing of the double vision: the ying-yang of the possible apocalypse to the tune of laughter in the land of Lunatophina; the exuberance of la marche à l'amour while wanting to be unnoticed and necessary. We endure the winter, but not in discontent. There are always "two people bending into the echo of their own laughter across a lake fresh with snow. 'And this, this,' one cries, looking back, 'is the whiteness of God's mind. Without us he is nothing.'" And with us, there is:

> Soudain ce goût de pomme
> et l'arbre dressé dans le milieu du monde
> quand les eaux font aux lunes contre poids
> et qu'ont fleuri les branches coronaires.

> Sudden tang of apples
> and the tree erect in the lap of the world
> while still waters counterpoise moons
> and coronary branches bloom.

## *Variation on the Word* Sleep

I would like to watch you sleeping,
which may not happen.
I would like to watch you,
sleeping. I would like to sleep
with you, to enter
your sleep as its smooth dark wave
slides over my head

and walk with you through that lucent
wavering forest of bluegreen leaves
with its watery sun & three moons
towards the cave where you must descend,
towards your worst fear

I would like to give you the silver
branch, the small white flower, the one
word that will protect you
from the grief at the centre
of your dream, from the grief
at the centre. I would like to follow
you up the long stairway
again & become
the boat that would row you back
carefully, a flame
in two cupped hands
to where your body lies
beside me, and you enter
it as easily as breathing in

I would like to be the air
that inhabits you for a moment
only. I would like to be that unnoticed
& that necessary.

## There are Delicacies

there are delicacies in you
   like the hearts of watches
there are wheels that turn
   on the tips of rubies
& tiny intricate locks

i need your help
   to contrive keys
there is so little time
   even for the finest
     watches

## Pumpkin: A Love Poem

Inside the pumpkin     I feel much better
I feel     loyalty to my pioneering
ancestors     I have entered

new territory     I feel a bit
sticky, yes cramped     but I feel
much better     trying to smile

I take out my knife     I cut
one triangular     hole
into the pale flesh     of my new

head     and then, gently
the tip of the knife     to my left
eyeball,     gently I twist

lift the old eye     to its new vision
of pea vines     snared in wire
and lettuce     gone to towering seed

and then     oh, what the hell
the second eye     no, not
quite yet     as blind as

love, I cut the new nose     flared
to demonstrate my     innate
ferocity     I slice off

my nose     and let it
sniff its way     into the scent of
staked tomatoes     and drying dill

I cut the new mouth     the place that
must be     toothed and jagged
the slit     that will

sneer     and then, about to
slice out    the old
I feel    on my pressing groin

the new mouth    on my cradled
like the seeds that    cradle
the new mouth    pressing

and then    squirming uneasily
inside the pumpkin    I am able
just barely    able to unzip

and she, outside    walking
in her garden    sees
my magnificent    unfallen

nature    my recovered ancestry
of borders    bravely crossed
and husbandry    triumphant

What are you doing    in my
pumpkin    she says, and I
muffled    sticky    humped

(I feel much better)    go
away, I shout    can't you see
at last    can't you see

leave me alone    (thrusting
with all my innate    ferocity)
at last, at last    can't you see
I'm fucking the whole world.

## Water and Marble

And shall I tell him that the thought of him
turns me to water
and when his name is spoken pale still sky
trembles and breaks and moves like blowing water
that winter thaws its frozen drifts in water
all matter blurs, unsteady, seen through water
and I, in him, dislimn, water in water?

As true: the thought of him
has made me marble
and when his name is spoken blowing sky
settles and freezes in a dome of marble
and winter seals its floury drifts in marble
all matter double-locks as dense as marble
and I, in other's eyes, am cut from marble.

## Fire and Water

'My lonely mother said the sun was a fire wheel
and leapt through the hoop,
fleeing on snowshoes
through snow thirty feet deep,
tangled her feet in the tops of trees
where she died
and was found in the spring
reaching for the earth,
her bones glazed by the wind,
and my father, so ashamed of his still-born sorrow,
went out and reached for the moon
reflected in a well
and drowned
believing he was born again.'

## La Fille maigre

Je suis une fille maigre
Et j'ai de beaux os.

J'ai pour eux des soins attentifs
Et d'étranges pitiés.

Je les polis sans cesse
Comme de vieux métaux.

Les bijoux et les fleurs
Sont hors de saison.

Un jour je saisirai mon amant
Pour m'en faire un reliquaire d'argent.

Je me pendrai
A la place de son cœur absent.

Espace comblé,
Quel est soudain en toi cet hôté sans fièvre?

Tu marches
Tu remues;
Chacun de tes gestes
Pare d'effroi la mort enclose.

Je reçois ton tremblement
Comme un don

Et parfois
En ta poitrine, fixée,
J'entr'ouvre
Mes prunelles liquides

Et bougent
Comme une eau verte
Des songes bizarres en enfantins.

## The Lean Girl

I am a lean girl
And I have beautiful bones.

I tend them with great care
And feel strange pity for them.

I continually polish them
As though they were old metal.

Now jewels and flowers
Are out of season.

One day I shall clasp my lover
And make of him a silver shrine.

I shall hang myself
In the place of his absent heart.

O well-filled space,
What is this cold guest suddenly in you?

You walk,
You move;
Each one of your gestures
Adorns with fear the enclosed death.

I receive your trembling
As a gift.

And sometimes
Fastened in your breast,
I half open
My liquid eyes

As strange and childish dreams
Swirl
Like green water.

*Translated by* F.R. SCOTT

## The Mushroom Factory

Mushrooms are the bald crowd
on their love beds
incubating in the gloom,
eating under their own rubber moons,
faceless gourmets
who believe God is an earthworm
in the land of tears
where the dead reappear
in an orgy, but no one is touching.

## God Loves Us Like Earthworms Love Wood


Try hard to make my words
more concerned with humans
less of the natural world
and my self-projection
coming through from the Sun
The moving figure casts a shadow
We are all starved creatures
gasping in the garden of vapours

Opened like a wine-skin
We last less than half-an-hour
The room is sharp
painfully in focus
Everything bold & square
The mail lies on the kitchen table
Water runs over the sink
The toilet is full with blood

Stroked by a corridor of light
the black cat sleeps on the bed

And the beautiful head is singing
My sorrow is a dried-up river
My love is a burnt pile of papers
My faith hovers in the light
by my closing eyes
My pity is for the living flowers
clotted in the humid air
pieces of bright red sponge

The beautiful head is singing
God loves us like earthworms love wood
long after the body is dead

## Love at Roblin Lake

My ambition as I remember and
I always remember was always
to make love vulgarly and immensely
     as the vulgar elephant doth
         & immense reptiles did
     in the open air openly
     sweating and grunting together
     and going
         "BOING     BOING     BOING"
                          making
every lunge a hole in the great dark
for summer cottagers to fall into at a later date
and hear inside faintly (like in a football
stadium when the home team loses)
ourselves still softly
     going
         *"boing     boing     boing"*
     as the vulgar elephant doth
         & immense reptiles did
in the star-filled places of earth
that I remember we left behind long ago
and forgotten everything after
on our journey into the dark

## Water and Worship: an open-air service on the Gatineau River

On the pathway mica glints.
Sun from the ripple-faceted water
shines, angled, to gray cliffs and the blue sky:
      from up here the boat-braided river is
      wind-riffled, fishes' meadows.
                But at
        eye-level, on the dock, the water looks deep,
             cold, black, cedar-sharp.
        The water is self-gulping under
        clefts and pier posts.
We listen.
your all-creating stillness, shining Lord,
trembles on our unknowing
             yearning
                 yielding lives:
      currents within us course
      as from released snow, rock-
      sluiced, slow welling from
          unexpected hidden springs,
      waters still acid,
      metallic with old wrecks —
        but Love draws near,
        cut-glass glory, shattering everything
               else in
        the one hope known:
        (how are You so
        at home with what we know?)
The waters lap.
Rocks contain and wait
in the strong sun.
        "Joyful, joyful, we adore Thee...."

## Confession

## Wart Hog

Moon-tusked, wrenching at roots,
I dream of women.

Once there were sacred boars
in the sacred woods,

eaters of corpses,
guardians of the groves

under the wand of the goddess.
Now I grub.

trample, and squeal,
bulk-shouldered, warted, haired

rank as the sweat of terror,
sour as shame,

guardian of no ritual
but the thrust

though darkness
of the bald horn of the moon.

## Moon Lines, After Jiménez

*Are you going around naked*
*in the house?*

                  speaking to moon

from the precise
place of darkness
speaking to
the unnamed woman

The moon has no shoes
undresses itself of cloud
river reflection

In dark bound rooms
the lost men imagine
paths of biography
on their palms

The greatest shipwrecks
are silent
semaphore their bones
through tide
they grow coloured history
wait
for the clock of moon

The abandoned woman
dives through darkness
and then
balances
with the magic fluid of her ear

It is here
it is now
when my thumb
swallows the candlelight

## The Dead Sky Letters

Love is a planet
made from the pulp
of what we dream.
I was never more alive

but the sky was against us,
a shining casket,
meteors burrowed
like maggots into our skin.

    \*\*\*

For a monument we cut
our initials into a tree trunk.
Whatever is carved from a living thing
fills in ... still
a sign, dear starthrower,

your scars in my skull.

    \*\*\*

Today I remember
how we pulled the blinds
and persuaded the universe
to come into our room,

planets rotating
around walls,
the Milky Way rising from the floor.

We were gods with mirror eyes
looking into each other's blindness.

    \*\*\*

Now this street into the night,
telephone poles
pointing to the Southern Cross.

Look up, dear blacksmith,
the nails are cold and sharp.

Remember the light, how it opened.
How we burst through.

    ***

Living in our moonshell,
the world seemed a small black stone.

What matters, you cried
is the space inside, the no-man's-land
between heart and mind.

What matters, I said, is what
comes up from the dead
and down from the boned air.

    ***

Sunday with its snares
and sparrows
hopping across the sill
on splintered legs.

Sunday, brighter than flowers
the new winter's blood
on the holly bush. The furnace hums:
sunlight under rock.
Keep pushing, dear snowheart,
each rebirth
we are more filled.

    ***

*I'll love you till*
*your heart's so fat,*
*cracks its shell*
*and scuttles*
*into the boiling vat.*

*I'll love you till*
*a peacock flies up your nose.*

*I'll love you till*
*your eyepit roots a blue rose*
*and your skin when we touch*
*secretes purple rainbows.*

*So keep the sun behind bars.*
*God's shadow, time, is a friend.*
*Our story's told in the stars.*
*Who cares when it ends.*

      \*\*\*

Wherever we went
white shadows of the drowned
floated across the sky.

We let go our bones
slipped into each other.
It was natural to be unbound

but love breaks
a wave leaving no message
except to swell and break again ...

my heart watching itself
I wait on the edge with my suitcase
of masks. No dream near
I shun the sun's revelations.

## Love Poem for Faye

Love is deep as a freshly killed bird
stroked by scimitars, measured by a whisker.
On everybody's doormat
there is a sleeping bird.

We want to forget
but still we feel the warmth. It hops on one leg
or hangs on a branch
with a broken wing.

## Connaissance

J'ai dans ma bouche le miel de ta bouche et de mon corps
       dans ton corps
O l'étrange pays ma belle étrangère de cet amour le nom
       que je ne connais pas de tes bras
Autour de mon cou comme la nuir pleine de femmes
       souveraines en cet étrange pays
Non ne parle pas laisse souffler le vent de ton souffle
       à mes lèvres
Ne parle pas sois à ta plainte toute mon oiselle ma captive
Et mon silence est dans tes yeux comme un corps étranger
       je roule dans l'eau de tes yeux
Je m'égare je te cherche et rôde dans la nielle de tes
       cheveux
Je m'absente en toi ô sommeil de l'homme ô maison de
       l'amour
Je meurs en toi je n'ai plus de visage que ton visage
       et voici que tu gémis de mourir en moi
Tu n'existes plus je n'existe plus nous sommes
       et d'une seule venue à notre nouveauté.

# Knowing

I have in my mouth the honey of your mouth
　　and of my body in your body
O strange country my beautiful stranger the name
　　of this love that I do not know from your arms
around my neck like a night full of women
　　regal in this strange country
No do not speak let the breath of your breath
　　breathe on my lips
Do not speak stay with your moans wholly my sparrow
　　my captive
And my silence is in your eyes like an unknown body
　　I am absorbed in the water of your eyes
I am lost and search and roam in the kernel
　　of your hair
I disappear in you O sleep of man O house of love
I die in you I have no face but your face and look
　　you are grieving to die in me
You no longer exist I no longer exist　　we are
　　and as one come to our newness.

*Translated by* F.R. SCOTT

## Lovers

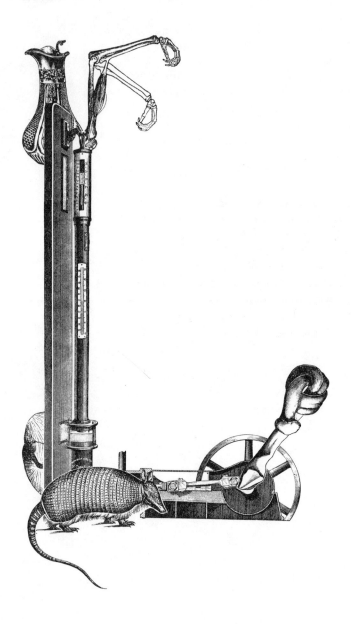

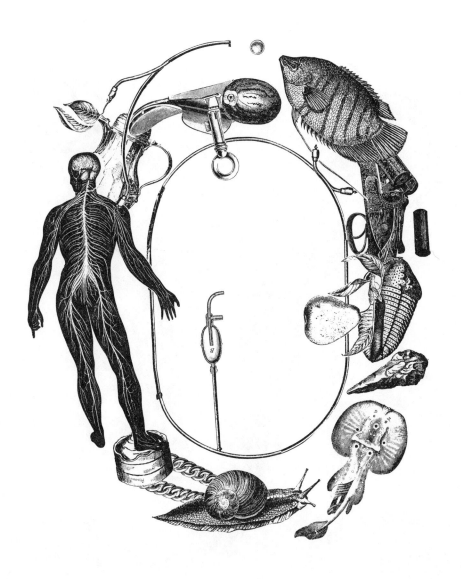

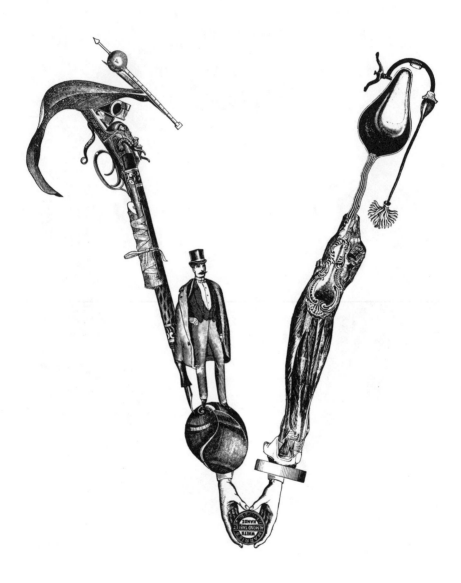

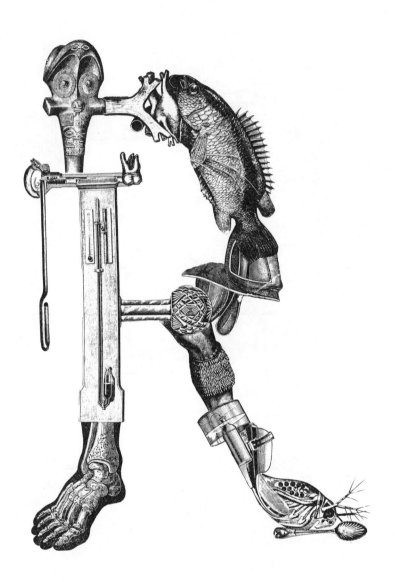

## An Old Niçoise Whore

The famous and rich, even the learned and the wise,
  Singly or in pairs went to her dwelling
To press their civilized lips to her thighs
  Or learn at first hand her buttocks' swelling.

Of high-paying customers she had no lack
  And was herself now rich: so she implied.
Mostly she had made her pile while on her back
  But sometimes she had made it on the side.

Reich she read; of course the Viennese doctor.
  Lawrence – his poems and novels she devoured;
Kafka at the beginning almost rocked her
  But as she read him more she said he soured.

Swedish she spoke, French, Polish, fluent German;
  Had even picked up Hindi – who knows how?
In bed she had learned to moan and sigh in Russian
  Though its rhythms troubled her even now.

A nymphomaniac like Napoleon's sister
  She could exhaust a bull or stallion;
Bankers had kneeled before her crotch to kiss her
  And ex-princes, Spanish and Italian.

And all the amorous mayors of France-Sud
  Impelled by lust or by regional pride
Would drive their Renaults into her neighbourhood,
  Ring her bell and troop happily inside.

And pimpled teenagers whom priests and rabbis
  Had made gauche, fearful, prurient and blind
Prodded by Venus had sought her expert thighs:
  Ah, to these she was especially kind.

And having translated several Swinburne lines
   She kept the finest whips she could afford
To be, though most aristocrats brought their canes,
   Ready for some forgetful English lord.

We saw waves like athletes dash towards the shore
   Breaking it seemed from a line of green scum;
We saw the sun dying, and this aged whore
   Noted how it gave clouds a tinge of rum.

Engaging was her mien, her voice low and sweet;
   Convent nuns might have envied her address.
She was touched by the bathers below her feet;
   I, by this vitality sprung from cess.

And as she spoke to me on the crowded quay
   And reminisced about her well-spent years
I mourned with her her shrivelled face and body
   And gave what no man had given her: tears.

## Eurynome II

Come all old maids that are squeamish
And afraid to make mistakes,
Don't clutter your lives up with boyfriends:
The nicest girls marry snakes.

If you don't mind slime on your pillow
And caresses as gliding as ice
– Cold skin, warm heart, remember,
And besides, they keep down the mice –

If you're really serious-minded,
It's the best advice you can take:
No rumpling, no sweating, no nonsense,
Oh who would not sleep with a snake?

## Walking

I walk into the room where you are standing behind a table.
The light in the room is pale yellow. There are no curtains.
The yellow is like the yellow of straw or very pale lemon.
You are wearing a loose wine-coloured top and a brown skirt.
I stand in front of the table with some red and blue flowers
in my hands and the cannon bone of a wild horse.
You spread out your papers on the desk and face the wall.
The cannon bone of the horse is white: Wheeaeah, Wheeaeah.
Another woman walks into the room and stands behind me.
The woman is naked and the tips of her breasts are pale red.
You begin drawing white suns on the blackboard.
One of the windows in the room is open and there are green
leaves against the cement. Some children are playing football.
You walk straight through the blackboard of white suns.
The cannon bone of the horse snuffles and blows air
through its cheeks. I turn around to face the hall where
you are standing with your back to me: naked except for a brown
tweed jacket which you undo and knot at your waist.
The second woman is standing in the hallway facing you
in a pink formal with a stuffed deer slung over her shoulder.
You turn to face me with your breasts gleaming like white suns.
The woman behind you is singing an old song about corn whiskey.
You are eating the red and blue flowers.
I am eating the white cannon bone of the horse.

## Gray John

*Gray John*
*When your time is up*
*who will tell you*
*she is gone?*

Everyone said Gray John was good with animals
yet he went to jail for fucking his horse
behind the barn and there was no-one
to tell him he wasn't alone;

three small boys hiding in the hay
entranced as he balanced on two sawhorses,
crooning, stroking her flanks.

Everyone said Gray John was a good man.
He minded his own and now he's in Riverview.
I haven't seen him for a year now
but I saw her today dragging in great circles

a plow over the spring ground
while her new master's whip hovered above her,
her flanks shuddering.

## Personal Landscape

Where the bog ends, there, where the ground lips, lovely
is love, not lonely.
                    Land is
love, round with it, where the hand is;
wide with love, cleared scrubland, grain
on a coin.
Oh, the wheat-field, the rock-bound rubble;
the untouched hills
                    as a thigh smooth;
the meadow.
Not only the poor soil lovely, the outworn prairie,
but the green upspringing,
the lark-land,
the promontory.

A lung-born land, this,
a breath spilling,
scanned by the valvular heart's
field glasses.

## An Iliad for His Summer Sweetheart

*And if she play with me with her shirt off,*
*We shall construct many Iliads.*
  *– E.P., Homage to Sextus Propertius*


I love to see my Amaryllis toss her shirt
  Away and kick her panties off, and loll,
  Languid and lazy, by the lily pool,
While old Silenius leers and laughing Cupids squirt.

My fancies swarm like bees about her golden head
  And golden thighs, where love's best ore is found.
  When she sinks softly to the sun-warmed ground
We need no silken walls, no blinds, no feather bed.

LEONARD COHEN

# For Anne

With Annie gone,
Whose eyes to compare
With the morning sun?

Not that I did compare,
But I do compare
Now that she's gone.

## I Loved Thee, Atthis

I loved thee, Atthis, in the long ago,
When the great oleanders were in flower
In the broad herded meadows full of sun.
And we would often at the fall of dusk
Wander together by the silver stream,
When the soft grass-heads were all wet with dew
And purple-misted in the fading light.
And joy I knew and sorrow at thy voice,
And the superb magnificence of love –
The loneliness that saddens solitude,
And the sweet speech that makes it durable –
The bitter longing and the keen desire,
The sweet companionship through quiet days
In the slow ample beauty of the world,
And the unutterable glad release
Within the temple of the holy night.
O Atthis, how I loved thee long ago
In that fair perished summer by the sea!

## ... Person, or A Hymn on and to the Holy Ghost

How should I find speech
to you, the self-effacing
whose other self was seen
alone by the only one,

to you whose self-knowing
is perfect, known to him,
seeing him only, loving
with him, yourself unseen?

Let the one you show me
ask you, for me,
you, all but lost in
the one in three,

to lead *my* self, effaced
in the known Light,
to be in him released
from facelessness,

so that where you
(unseen, unguessed, liable
to grievous hurt) would go
I may show him visible.

## Wind-Chimes in a Temple Ruin

This is the moment
   for two glass leaves
dangling dumb
   from the temple eaves
This is the instant
   when the sly air breathes
and the tremblers touch
   where no man sees
Who is the moving
   or moved is no matter
but the birth of the possible
   song in the rafter
that dies as the wind goes
   nudging other
broken eaves
   for waiting lovers

## Arcanum One: The Prince

and in the morning the king loved you most
and wrote your name with a sun and a beetle
and a crooked ankh, and in the morning
you wore gold mainly, and the king adorned you
with many more names

beside fountains, both of you slender
as women, circled and walked together
like bracelets circling water, both of you
slender as women, wrote your names with
beetles and with suns, and spoke together
in the golden mornings

and the king entered your body
into the bracelet of his name
and you became a living syllable
in his golden script, and your body
escaped from me like founting water
all the daylong

but in the evenings you wrote my name
with a beetle and a moon, and lay upon me
like a long broken necklace which had fallen
from my throat and the king loved you
most in the morning, and his glamourous love
lay lengthwise along us all the evening.

## Arcanum Four: The Embalming

along your body strips of gold unroll
your name which caused a kingdom's fall
and your warped ribs, my silent one,
refuse the sun, and down your legs run
legends of the night, in white cloth I wound you
in your final house beside the water
and I know the gates are locked forever,
the gates of light are locked forever
as my loins lock, as the river.

in white cloth bound, and blind
you breathe in death the winds of night
as the sweet stiff corpse of your petrified
sex points upward into heaven
in your tomb beside the river,
though the gates of light are locked forever,
the legs and lips of light are locked forever.

my fingers twice have traced
your name all down your flesh, and they
have dipped its signs in water.
now sleep my blind, my silent brother
as my womb locks, as the river,
your tomb a virgin by jackals sealed
and the gates of light are locked forever.

## Arcanum Seven: The Return

now as I wear around my neck a necklace
of a million suns, you come
undead, unborn, thou Ghost of the morning!

I notice that you wear our father's ring
but I must say no more
for the bed of ebony and straw
lies like a fallen song upon the floor
where last we left it, broken with love and bare.
the world will loathe our love of salt and fire
and none will let you call me sister here.

see how my body bears the mouthmarks made
in times long past, star-wounds in night unhealed;
since then it was a cave by jackals sealed.
but now my legs are once more cages
for a great far-flying bird, my breasts
small pyramids of love, my mouth
is empty of the dark wine of my waiting.

O tell me all the things you saw,
and call me sister
and bless this bed of ebony and straw.

## Necropsy of Love

If it came about you died
it might be said I loved you:
love is an absolute as death is,
and neither bears false witness to the other –
But you remain alive.

No, I do not love you
              hate the word,
that private tyranny inside a public sound,
your freedom's yours and not my own:
but hold my separate madness like a sword,
and plunge it in your body all night long.

If death shall strip our bones of all but bones,
then here's the flesh, and flesh that's drunken-sweet
as wine cups in deceptive lunar light:
reach up your hand and turn the moonlight off,
and maybe it was never there at all,
so never promise anything to me:
but reach across the darkness with your hand,
reach across the distance of tonight,
and touch the moving moment once again
              before you fall asleep –

LEONARD COHEN

## As the Mist Leaves No Scar

As the mist leaves no scar
On the dark green hill,
So my body leaves no scar
On you, nor ever will.

When wind and hawk encounter,
What remains to keep?
So you and I encounter,
Then turn, then fall to sleep.

As many nights endure
Without a moon or star,
So will we endure
When one is gone and far.

# 1 2 3 4 5 6 7 8 9 K. O.

```
M M M M M M M M M M M M M M M M M M M M M M M M M M M M M M
M                                                          M
M                                                          M
M          1 2 3 4 5 6 7 8 9 K. O.                         M
M                                                          M
M          yin l'épine se pique à tout pore épilé net      M
M          par le napalM supplante les poils du soldat     M
M                                                          M
M          à l'aube les barbelés bardent sa peau en plaies M
M          d'une pelure de porc-épic ou de cactus en Métal M
M                                                          M
M          le Mon corps n'est MêMe plus attaqué à l'aube   M
M          par les épines de roses de ronces d'aubépines   M
M                                                          M
M          le soleil ne s'est MêMe pas hissé à l'horizon   M
M          ce sont les fleurs de feu qui fleurissent et    M
M          lèchent la nuit de leurs longues larges langues M
M          et les boulets de la Mitraille alluMent l'aube et M
M          ô le ballet du blessé d'une trop vive luMière   M
M          ainsi lovée autour des chairs ainsi qu'une aube M
M          il traîne son buisson ardent coMMe un boulet    M
M          à l'aube son corps igné avale la nuit le dévore M
M          lui-MêMe croques ses lèvres dans son cri pris   M
M          les avions levant le vent le feu s'énerve vite  M
M          il y a pénurie d'eau dans les barbelés sol sec  M
M          toute terre est toujours un tapis d'épines et et M
M                                                          M
M          naître par l'épine de la verge par sa rosée et et M
M          à l'aube dans la rossée d'obus Mourir béat et et et M
M          bardé de barbelés protège l'espace de ta vie M M M M
M                                                          M
M                                                          M
M M M M M M M M M M M M M M M M M M M M M M M M M M M M M M
```

## 1 2 3 4 5 6 7 8 9 K. O.

```
M M M M M M M M M M M M M M M M M M M M M M M M M M M M M M
M                                                          M
M                                                          M
M    1 2 3 4 5 6 7 8 9 K. O.                                M
M                                                          M
M    yin the thorn stings at every pore plucked clean      M
M    by napalM supplants the soldier's hairs               M
M                                                          M
M    at dawn the barbed wire tears his skin into wounds    M
M    of porcupine hide or of Molten cactus                 M
M                                                          M
M    the soft body is attacked no longer by dawn           M
M    by rose prickles braMble hawthorns                    M
M                                                          M
M    the sun did not even hoist itself on the horizon      M
M    it is the flowers of fire that flower and             M
M    lick the night with their long large lips             M
M    and the Machine-gun bullets illuMinate the dawn and   M
M    o the ballet of those battered by too bright blaze    M
M    thus coiled about flesh like dawn                     M
M    he drags his burning bush like a bullet               M
M    at dawn his ignited body swallows night devours hiM   M
M    he hiMself Munches his lips in captive cry            M
M    the airplanes lift the wind the fire sputters quickly M
M    there is a draft aMong the barbed wires parched soil  M
M    all earth is always a carpet of thorns and and        M
M                                                          M
M    to be born by the penis-thorn by its dew and and      M
M    at dawn in the thrashing of shells to die sMugly and and and  M
M    barbed by barbed wire protect the space of your life M M M  M
M                                                          M
M                                                          M
M M M M M M M M M M M M M M M M M M M M M M M M M M M M M M
```

*Translated by* JOHN ROBERT COLOMBO

## The Day Aviva Came to Paris

The day you came naked to Paris
The tourists returned home without their guidebooks,
The hunger in their cameras finally appeased.

Alone once more with their gargoyles, the Frenchmen
Marvelled at the imagination that had produced them
And once again invited terror into their *apéritifs*.
Death was no longer exiled to the cemeteries.

In their royal gardens where the fish die of old age,
They perused something else besides newspapers
– A volume perhaps by one of their famous writers.
They opened their hearts to let your tender smile defrost them;
Their livers filled with an unassuageable love of justice.
They became the atmosphere around them.

They learned to take money from Americans
Without a feeling of revulsion towards them;
And to think of themselves
As not excessively subtle or witty.
"*Au diable* with Voltaire," they muttered,
"Who was a national calamity.
*Au diable* with *la République*.
(A race of incurable *petit bourgeois*, the French
Are happiest under a horse under a man.)
*Au diable* with *la Monarchie*!
We saw no goddesses during either folly;
Our bald-headed savants never told us
Such a blaze of pubic hair anywhere existed."
And they ordered the grandson of Grandma Moses
To paint it large on the dome of le Sacré-Cœur.

My little one, as if under those painted skies
It was again 1848,
They leaped as one mad colossal Frenchman from their *café*
        Pernods
Shouting, "*Vive l'Australienne*!
*Vive* Layton who brought her among us!
Let us erect monuments of black porphyry to them!
Let us bury them in the Panthéon!"
(*Pas si vite, messieurs*; we are still alive.)

And when, an undraped Jewish Venus,
You pointed to a child, a whole slum starving in her eyes,
Within earshot of the Tuileries,
The French who are crazy or catholic enough
To place, facing each other, two tableaux
– One for the Men of the Convention, and one puffing the Orators
        of the Restoration –
At once made a circle wide as the sky around you
While the Mayor of the 5th *Arondissement*
Addressed the milling millions of Frenchmen:

"See how shapely small her adorable ass is;
Of what an incredible pink rotundity each cheek.
*A bas* Merovingian and Valois!
*A bas* Charlemagne and Henri Quatre!
For all the adulations we have paid them
In our fabulous *histoires*
They cannot raise an erection between them. Ah,
For too long has the madness of love
Been explained to us by sensualists and curés.
*A bas* Stendhal! *A bas* Bossuet!

"Forever and forever, from this blazing hour
All Paris radiates from Aviva's nest of hair
– Delicate hatchery of profound delights –
From her ever-to-be adored Arche de Triomphe!
All the languors of history
Take on meaning clear as a wineglass or the belch of an angel
Only if thought of as rushing
On the wings of a rhinoceros towards this absorbing event.
Voyeurs, voyez! The moisture of her instep
Is a pool of love
Into which sheathed in candy-paper
Anaesthetized politicians drop from the skies!"
(Word jugglery of course, my Sweet; but the French love it
– Mistake it in fact for poetry)

And the applaudissements and bravos
Bombinating along the Boulevard Saint-Germain
Make the poor docile Seine
Think our great Atlantic was upon it.
It overflowed with fright into the bookstalls
And sidewalk cafés.
Fifteen remaining Allemands with their cameras
Were flushed down the Rue Pigalle.

And when you were raised up
Into my hairy arms by the raving emotional crowds
Waving frenzied bottles of Beaujolais
And throwing the corks away ecstatically
(Not saving them!)
It was my Love, my Darling,
As if someone had again ordered an advance
Upon the Bastille
Which we recalled joyously, face to face at last,
Had yielded after only a small token resistance.

# from Boucliers mégalomanes

Mon Olivine
Ma Ragamuche
je te stoptatalère sur la bouillette mirkifolchette
J'aracramuze ton épaulette
Je crudimalmie ta ripanape
Je te cruscuze
Je te goldèple
Ouvre tout grand ton armomacabre
et laisse le jour entrer dans tes migmags
O Lunèthophyne
je me penche et te cramuille
Ortie déplépojdèthe
j'agrimanche ta rusplète
Et dans le désert des marquemacons tes seins obèrent le silence

# from Megalomaniac Shields

My Olivine
My Ragamoosh
i stoptiskateez you on the sillybead slowboil
I tearacramulche your epaulette
I roughamumple your reepanappy
I crouscouz you
I galdapple you
Open wide your armoimacabre
and let the sun shine into your migmags
Oh Lunatophina
i bend down and cramble you
Deplepodated sting-nettle
i agributt your rusplette
And in the desert of markmasons your breasts burden
    the silence.

*Translated by* RAY ELLENWOOD

## Fecundity

I'm a walled orchard.
Fruit swells
inflamed by the evening.

I ache for your bite,
to have water, fire,
sucked from me.
Outside the gates
I hear swans rutting.

I want to be pinned
to the hot earth,
my cry splitting
the moon, juice and seed.

God, how I long for stars
to mark where
I've taken you in.

## Gray Silk Twisting

I stick my tongue in you,
move like a great fluid worm
eating out your soul. At night
I was told our souls leave our bodies
through our mouths
but I know it leaves every hole
like gray silk twisting,
tasting of earth.

I enter you this way,
my eyes in your hair,
my fingers gripping the smooth
lips of you. Without speaking
you wrap your gray inside me
as I dance
finally thigh to thigh
attached to you by hooks,
tearing me as I come.

## The Garden of the Sexes

I have a garden closed away
And shadowed from the light of day
Where Love hangs bound on every tree
And I alone go free.

His sighs, that turn the weathers round,
His tears, that water all the ground,
His blood, that reddens in the vine,
These all are mine.

At night the golden apple-tree
Is my fixed station, whence I see
Terrible, sublime and free,
My loves go wheeling over me.

## Bartok and the Geranium

She lifts her green umbrellas
Towards the pane
Seeking her fill of sunlight
Or of rain;
Whatever falls
She has no commentary
Accepts, extends,
Blows out her furbelows,
Her bustling boughs;

And all the while he whirls
Explodes in space,
Never content with this small room:
Not even can he be
Confined to sky
But must speed high and higher still
From galaxy to galaxy,
Wrench from the stars their momentary notes
Steal music from the moon.

She's daylight
He is dark
She's heaven-held breath
He storms and crackles
Spits with hell's own spark.

Yet in this room, this moment now
These together breathe and be:
She, essence of serenity,
He in a mad intensity
Soars beyond sight
Then hurls, lost Lucifer,
From heaven's height.

And when he's done, he's out:
She leans a lip against the glass
And preens herself in light.

## Communication

Femme elle se mêlait nue aux fougères,
ses poils accueillant bien les papillons.
Sous elle j'étais son humus son nourricier obscur,
le musicien de ses nervures.
D'or de vert et de transparence je la sevrais.
Ma vie en elle montait jusqu'à son âme.

## Communion

Naked, she wove herself into the ferns
her hair a glad welcome for butterflies.
I was her rich mould, her hidden nutriment
the musician of her strings.
I set her apart from the gold the green the
   transparency.
My life in her shone out from her very eyes.

*Translated by* F.R. SCOTT

from ARIONE

SOMETIMES WE SPENT WHOLE DAYS...

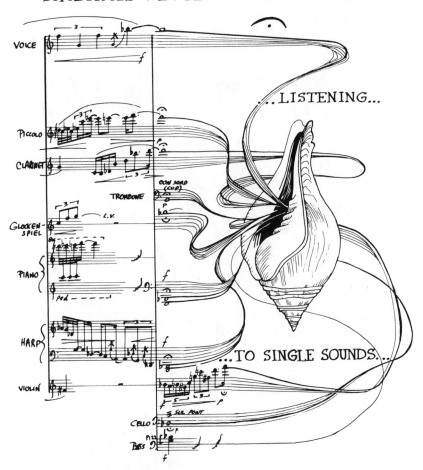

...LISTENING...

...TO SINGLE SOUNDS...

SOMETIMES WE SPENT WHOLE DAYS
REPEATING ONE WORD, GRADUALLY
REVEALING NEW ASPECTS OF ITS
MEANING...

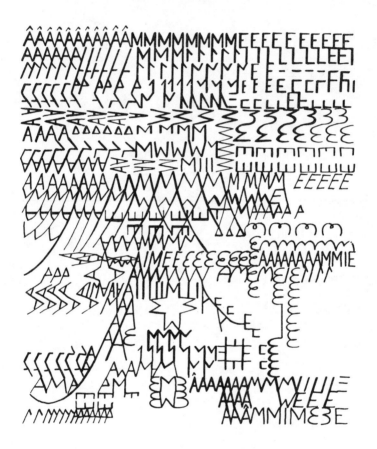

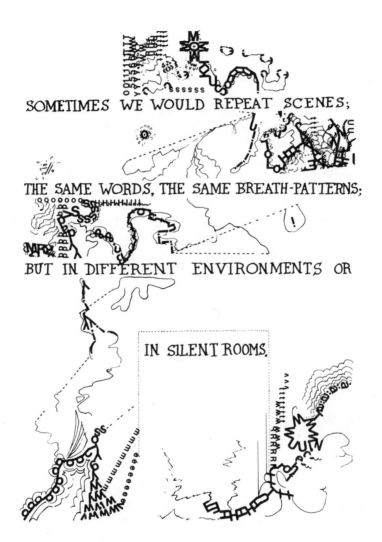

SOMETIMES WE WOULD REPEAT SCENES;

THE SAME WORDS, THE SAME BREATH-PATTERNS;

BUT IN DIFFERENT ENVIRONMENTS OR

IN SILENT ROOMS.

SOMETIMES WE WOULD REPEAT SCENES;

THE SAME WORDS, THE SAME BREATH-PATTERNS;

BUT IN DIFFERENT ENVIRONMENTS OR

IN SILENT ROOMS.

SOMETIMES WE WOULD REPEAT SCENES;

THE SAME WORDS, THE SAME BREATH-PATTERNS,

BUT IN DIFFERENT ENVIRONMENTS OR

IN SILENT ROOMS.

...OR IN SILENT ROOMS.

## Kate

I

She laughs with all, but none hath seen her weep,
A tender stoic, beautiful and wise.
What sorrow or what passion she may keep
Behind that full pale brow, those veiled grey eyes
I know not, none shall know; but all the tide
Of all her being is softly set to truth.
In brow and breast and dainty foot abide
The strength of woman's years, the grace of youth.

What gentle power, I wonder, in her moods
Sustains her, what unvexed philosophy;
For when I think of her, I seem to see
April herself among the sunny woods
With laughing brooks and little clouds that pass;
I dream of bluebirds and hepaticas.

II

There is no single hour for me, no place
Untouched by her bright presence, nobly sweet –
The slender form, so deftly made for grace,
From the wise forehead to the winged feet –
The beautiful broad brow, so soft and full,
Above the tender eyelids and grey eyes,
Where gleams of artless laughter break and lull,
And sparkling tears and such deep mysteries

Of mind and spirit as the kind grave lips
Leave speechless for the kindred sense to learn.
To her, forever, like sea-stained ships
To the old havens, all my thoughts return –
Return, and lie close moored – to rest a while
By some stored look or some remembered smile.

*November 10, 1895*

## from Le Vierge incendié

tu étais cette main        cette marche douce dans les cous le soir        les jardins versicolores et les maisons sises au bord des yeux        tous les paysages sont derrière les maisons        montagnes poilues        baisers sur les seins quand il pleut        c'est l'automne le vent qui t'arrache à l'arbre du sommeil        on a des amours écartelées et des mains de rhubarbe        on a des pages closes des corps épuisés        la neige va tomber        c'est mourir avec le parterre        on deviendra la nuit blanche du vide        juste à regarder passer l'eau dans la glace        on connaît le chemin        on s'en rend compte tout à coup        quand le soleil est mort personne ne veut plus mourir        où aller quand on avait été si bien avec les arbres et les bêtes

jambe avec le pied le mollet le genou et la cuisse et le ventre en haut chatte        petite jambe chaude et soie de frisson et l'autre jambe        les deux jambes et les deux mains sur les deux jambes        et tout le long des deux jambes        et le ventre au bout des jambes et les seins et les épaules et les bras d'épaules avec les mains au bout        et la tête avec la bouche        et les paupières et les cheveux sur les temps        tout un corps        toute une femme        tout l'autre corps et le mien        les deux miens        l'autre        celui qui n'est pas le mien et qui est le mien

## from The Virgin Burned

you were this hand    this gentle stroll in the hollows of the neck at
evening    the patchwork gardens and the houses at the corner of
the eye    all landscapes are behind the houses    hairy mountains
    kisses on the breasts when it rains    it's autumn the wind that
tears you from the tree of sleep    we have sundered loves and rhubarb
hands    we have closed pages exhausted bodies    it's going to snow
    it's a matter of dying with the flower beds    we will become the
white noise of the void    watching the water move in the icy mirror
    we know the way    it comes to us all at once    when the sun
is dead no one wants to die any more    where to go when we've been
so much at home with the trees and the animals

*Translated by* D.G. JONES

leg with foot    calf    knee    and thigh    and belly above
pussy little warm leg and shiver of silk and other leg    two legs and
two hands on two legs    and all along two legs    and belly at end
of legs and breasts and shoulders    and arms with hands at end
and head with mouth    and eyelids and hair on forehead    a whole
body a whole woman    a whole other body and mine both mine
the other    one which is not mine and which is mine

*Translated by* LARRY SHOULDICE

## Slowly I Married Her

Slowly I married her
Slowly and bitterly married her love
Married her body
    in boredom and joy
Slowly I came to her
Slow and resentfully came to her bed
Came to her table
in hunger and habit
    came to be fed
Slowly I married her
sanctioned by none
with nobody's blessings
in nobody's name
    amid general warnings
    amid general scorn
Came to her fragrance
    my nostrils wide
Came to her greed
    with seed for a child
Years in the coming
and years in retreat
    Slowly I married her
Slowly I kneeled
And now we are wounded
    so deep and so well
that no one can hurt us
except Death itself
    And all through Death's dream
I move with her lips
The dream is a night
    but eternal the kiss
And slowly I come to her
    slowly we shed
the clothes of our doubting
    and slowly we wed

## The Gift of Tongue

He lay on a shelf
of stone in the valley

of Kidron. It was
the dead of night.

His neighbors, scattered
among the weeds of

Olivet Hill, were common
headstones, their bones

the calligraphy of a final
hour. But he and his

woman were naked and
ignored the language

of moss along the bone,
and all grief, calumny,

fell from his eyes
when she knelt and gave him

the gift of tongue. So too,
the moon swallowed

the sun. His cry named
her and in reply

they heard the muezzin
in his minaret,

that stone shaft into
the mouth of god.

## Et je prierai ta grâce

Et je prierai ta grâce de me crucifier
Et de clouer mes pieds à ta montagne sainte
Pour qu'ils ne courent pas sur les routes fermées
Les routes qui s'en vont vertigineusement
De toi
Et que mes bras aussi soient tenus grands ouverts
À l'amour par des clous solides, et mes mains
Mes mains ivres de chair, brûlantes de péché,
Soient, à te regarder, lavées par ta lumière
Et je prierai l'amour de toi, chaîne de feu,
De me bien attacher au bord de ton calvaire
Et de garder toujours mon regard sur ta face
Pendant que reluira par-dessus ta douleur
Ta résurrection et le jour éternel.

## Et je prierai ta grâce

And I will entreat thee of thy grace to crucify me
And nail my feet unto thy holy mountain
So that they may not run upon forbidden roads
The roads that lead bewilderingly away
From thee
And so my arms should also be held wide open
To love by firm-fixed nails, and that my hands
My hands drunken with flesh, burning with sin,
Should be, beneath thy gaze, washed in thy light
And I will entreat thy love, a fiery chain,
To bind me fast beside thy calvary
And keep my gaze ever upon thy face
While still above thy suffering shall shine out
The resurrection and the light eternal.

*Translated by* JOHN GLASSCO

## The Cinnamon Peeler

If I were a cinnamon peeler
I would ride your bed
and leave the yellow bark dust
on your pillow.

Your breasts and shoulders would reek
you could never walk through markets
without the profession of my fingers
floating over you. The blind would
stumble certain of whom they approached
though you might bathe
under rain gutters, monsoon.

Here on the upper thigh
at this smooth pasture
neighbour to your hair
or the crease
that cuts your back. This ankle.
You will be known among strangers
as the cinnamon peeler's wife.

I could hardly glance at you
before marriage
never touch you
– your keen nosed mother, your rough brothers.
I buried my hands
in saffron, disguised them
over smoking tar,
helped the honey gatherers . . .

When we swam once
I touched you in water
and our bodies remained free,
you could hold me and be blind of smell.
You climbed the bank and said

this is how you touch other women
the grass cutter's wife, the lime burner's daughter.
And you searched your arms
for the missing perfume
                    and knew

          what good is it
to be the lime burner's daughter
left with no trace
as if not spoken to in the act of love
as if wounded without the pleasure of a scar.

You touched
your belly to my hands
in the dry air and said
I am the cinnamon
peeler's wife. Smell me.

## Coming of Age

The pit at midnight
crusty with snow
like day-old bread pudding

and Giffey the outlaw
giving a sermon about sin

right down there
in a preacher's black gown

only his cock and his
cloven hoof peeping out a little.

The chalk pit where
Giffey would show us his stump.
We used to line up for him,
undaunted by his obscene gestures.

And show him *our* proud bodies.

All nine of us, nubile and
cheeky, dancing just out of his
reach

and old Giffey getting all creamy
and churned up
with each of us worrying and wriggling
like that.

We were so quick
we teased him until he came,
blasting off into the moonlight
for all the world to watch.

Then he would cry
and we thought he was crazy,
not daring to come close or
touch, not near enough for
comfort.

We were the peaty source of his
darkness, with our lies and our smiles
and stories about our lives.
For there were no blessings in our cold
eyes, only cruelty, and more of that for
our youth.

At night I would dream of
giving myself to him,
being drilled into the dirt,
cursing and carrying on like
old Giffey himself when his
wormy thing wouldn't get hard.

I saw myself kneeling below him,
opening myself before him,
lying open beneath him

tightening and tempting

until one night he never
came anymore.

We were haunted and stripped
naked at last, eager for
whatever unpleasantness he would
permit

anxious for all his ungainliness:

he never came.

Colder than ever in that chalk
pit tracing circles with our toes

we crept home finally to our
clean beds, long past the usual
hour, completed and alone.

## Il y a certainement quelqu'un

Il y a certainement quelqu'un
Qui m'a tuée
Puis s'en est allé
Sur la pointe des pieds
Sans rompre sa danse parfaite.

A oublié de me coucher
M'a laissée debout
Toute liée
Sur le chemin
Le cœur dans son coffret ancien
Les prunelles pareilles
A leur plus pure image d'eau

A oublié d'effacer la beauté du monde
Autour de moi
A oublié de fermer mes yeux avides
Et permis leur passion perdue.

## There is Certainly Someone

There is certainly someone
Who once killed me
And then walked away
On the tip of his toes
Without breaking his perfect dance.

Who forgot to put me to bed
And left me standing
All tightly bound
On the road
My heart sealed up as before
My two eyes like
Their own pure image of water

Who forgot to erase the beauty of the world
Around me
Forgot to close my hungry eyes
And permitted their wasted passion.

*Translated by* F.R. SCOTT

## Gray Glove

Among branches
a bird lands fluttering,
a soft gray glove
with a heart.

The land at twilight.
Swamp of black mist.
A first planet. A swordtip.
The bird chanting
in a jail of darkness.

This is the last unclassified bird,
the one one never sees,
but hears when alone, walking.

You can see how far I've gone
not to speak of you.
Birds have made a simple bargain
with the land.

The only song I know
is the one I see with my eyes,
the one I'd give up my eyes
in order for you to hear.

## Flic

full clouds
across the sky
and shadows chase
the hills

the sky a pinto
bright blue pony.

If you get on the sky
I'll take your picture

as when we lay
            in afterlove
making movies
on our eyelids
in colour

**Blues**

## L'Aube ensevelie

Plus bas encore mon amour taisons-nous
Ce fruit ouvert dans le soleil
Tes yeux comme l'haleine de l'aurore
Comme le sel des buissons révélateurs

Taisons-nous taisons-nous il y a quelque part
Un cœur qui pleure sur un cœur
Pour la dernière aventure
Pour le déchirement total

Taisons-nous rien ne peut recommencer
Il faut oublier les lampes les heures sacrées
Il faut oublier les faux feux du jour
Notre délice nous foudroie

Plus bas encore mon amour
Ah plus bas mon cher amour
Ces choses doivent être murmurées
Comme entre deux mourants

Bientôt nous ne voudrons plus distinguer
La frange des rides sur nos fronts
Ah regardons bondir les étoiles
Aux justes secrets de nos doigts

Regardons ce que refuse
L'or détruit du souvenir
La belle chambre insolite
Et ses bras d'éclairs sourds

Taisons-nous oublions tout
Noyons les mots magiques
Préparons nos tendres cendres
Pour le grand silence inexorable

## The Shrouded Dawn

Still softer my love    let us hush
This fruit laid open in the sun
Your eyes    like the breath of dawn
Like the salt of telltale shrubbery

Let us hush let us hush there is somewhere
A heart that weeps upon a heart
For the very last adventuring
And for the total severance

Let us hush    nothing can begin again
We must forget the lamps the holy hours
We must forget the day's false fires
For our delight annihilates us

Still softer then    softer my love
Ah still my dear love
These matters are for murmuring
As between two dying things

Soon we shall no more wish to trace
The fringe of wrinkles on our brows
Ah let us watch the stars leap
At the just secrets of our fingertips

Let us remark what is refused
By the ruined gold of memory
The lovely unaccustomed room
And its dull lightning arms

Let us hush now and forget it all
Let us drown the magic words
Let us prepare our tender embers
For the great inexorable calm

*Translated by* PETER MILLER

## It Was Never Like This Before

I don't want to get up in the morning
the dreams are becoming more intense;
the vivid reds are boiling in my brain
erupting through a purple sky.

Leaves bury my fantasies:
I'm in a russet pond full of virgins;
their skin is the white of lilies
they want to make love under water.

The women have glowing turquoise eyes
small half-lemon breasts
& inoffensive thighs, smooth
like the arcs of doves in the blank.

I wear a smile like an old suit –
the dreams are becoming more intimate;
I'm afraid of the orange sunset
it will impregnate the ladies.

The virgins of the deep extend their arms
their raspberry nipples flash in the sunflower light
but morning hauls me up
up toward the earth, & another day.

## "From Sex, This Sea"

From sex, this sea, we have emerged
into a quiet room
our bodies bare

We have been washed by tides
the glacial waters welling up
to shudder and subside, the broad streams

wandering to the pole

The climate of the flesh
is temperate here
though we look out on a winter world

We are the islanders
between two seasons, and a garden where
we are the botanists

of our own flowers. And yet

I am led into the winter air
by certain nameless twigs, as bare
as we are. I would find

them also in our mouths

## White Room

dear thin lady
you bend over your stomach
and your body is cool fruit

skin covers stray bones on your back
as sand envelops scattered fragments
of a wrecked aircraft

You are bending over your stomach
I am descending
like helicopters onto the plain

and we collapse
as flesh
within the angles of the room

## Now Of Sleeping

Under her grandmother's patchwork quilt
a calico bird's-eye view
of crops and boundaries
naming dimly the districts of her body
sleeps my Annie like a perfect lady

Like ages of weightless snow
on tiny oceans filled with light
her eyelids enclose deeply
a shade tree of birthday candles
one for every morning
until the now of sleeping

The small banner of blood
kept and flown by Brother Wind
long after the pierced bird fell down
is like her red mouth
among the squalls of pillow

Bearers of evil fancy
of dark intention and corrupting fashion
who come to rend the quilt
plough the eye and ground the mouth
will contend with mighty Mother Goose
and Farmer Brown and all good stories
of invincible belief
which surround her sleep
like the golden weather of a halo

Well-wishers and her true lover
may stay to watch my Annie
sleeping like a perfect lady

under her grandmother's patchwork quilt
but they must promise to whisper
and to vanish by morning –
all but her one true lover.

## Lady, Lady

Lady, lady, I cannot lie,
I didn't cut down your cherry tree.

It was another man, in another season,
for the same reason.

I eat the stone and not the flesh,
it is the bare bone of desire I want,

something you would throw a dog,
or me, though I insult by saying so.

God knows it is not said
of your body, that it is like

a bone thrown to a dog
or that I would throw it away, which

moment to moment I cannot remember
under those baggy clothes you wear –

which, if I love and tell,
I love well.

## Proteus and Nymph

I put down my book
   and stare at the distant haze;
the loud-voiced Greeks around me
   chomping on their fish and *peponi*
must reckon I'm having age-old thoughts
   on the human condition.
Noisy fools. I'm thinking of the waves
   gently cupping the breasts
of the lovely nymph just risen from the sea
   and the water lapping
her thighs and her delicate love-cleft

When she swims away
   she pulls my thoughts after her
in watery streaks of light. I become
   the sea around her
and she nestles in my long green arms
   or is held in the flowing
wavelets of my white hair. I billow
   above her like a dolphin
stroke her limbs and nip her rosy neck and shoulders
   with sharp unceasing kisses
till languorously she slips to the ribbed sand
   where under the haloing starfish
fern weed and enamoured seasnake I quiver
   between her silver thighs

## These Poems, She Said

These poems, these poems,
these poems, she said, are poems
with no love in them. These are the poems of a man
who would leave his wife and child because
they made noise in his study. These are the poems
of a man who would murder his mother to claim
the inheritance. These are the poems of a man
like Plato, she said, meaning something I did not
comprehend but which nevertheless
offended me. These are the poems of a man
who would rather sleep with himself than with women,
she said. These are the poems of a man
with eyes like a drawknife, with hands like a pickpocket's
hands, woven of water and logic
and hunger, with no strand of love in them. These
poems are as heartless as birdsong, as unmeant
as elm leaves, which if they love love only
the wide blue sky and the air and the idea
of elm leaves. Self-love is an ending, she said,
and not a beginning. Love means love
of the thing sung, not of the song or the singing.
These poems, she said . . .
                    You are, he said,
beautiful.
          That is not love, she said rightly.

# from Carnival

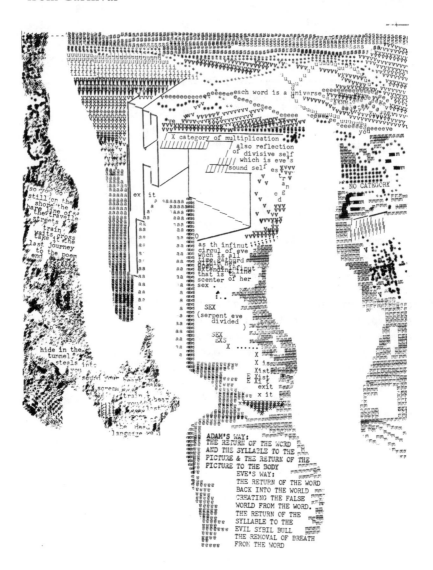

say like the red outline
of beginning ADAM

TEMPTATION COMES IN TWO
FORMS ONLY:THE LINEAR
AND THE CIRCULAR
BUT ALL TRUE GAMES
ARE VISIONS
AND TRUE VISION
IS RADIAL

ahAH
deadly ser-pe

## i should have begun with your toes

with maybe just the little one
so clean & succulent
so tiny
it's no toe at all
but a spare nipple        ummmm

now the big one?
big? the nail on it so weeny
& silvery
it's more like a stamp-hinge
to hold down some rarity
a pink imperforate
engraved in *taille douce*

& you've got ten
all in mint condition

& now let's forget
philately
& up the golden stairs!

## Invocation

You loved one, hurt one, loving one still strong . . .
If you were only an impossible vision
Why should you lurk – a quiet worm in my tongue
Wait and live to raise this invocation?
What did you look through, in Spook Canyon
Besides that smiling mask, carved from a tree –
Tools learning as they cut a growing wisdom
To top and ornament your poor wronged body?
You have entered me, dead but not done.

I've loved, and love the Earth. If you are Death
Stay around to summon more performance.
Is that smile kinder yet? Plumbing consent?
Wait for the laughter! It'll blow breath
Tumbling all your atoms to collect 'em
Till lungs pump, your heart flutters, eyes go wide
And I'll be wise, at last, to find a bride.
My vehicle accelerates, bright one. Come.

## L'Acte de l'œil au mauve

*« Des amantes ont vu leur œil devenir l'œil de leur amante au loin. »*
MONIQUE WITTIG, SANDE ZEIG

Comme pour entamer le vertige, la version lisse des épaules de corps amantes ou s'y retrouver au risque vivant de la lucidité enlacées fameuses et proches comme une musique. Ce soir, je repasse dans ma tête l'écume et ma bouche pour que toutes deux partagées à nourrir le sens nous y retrouvions plus fort que le vent la sensation des abeilles, nous exhortant dans un jardin. Lentement cela passait par l'œil, un sérum, vitale de l'une à l'autre. Perturbées, nouvelle conjoncture, dans un cycle ou franchir importe seulement quand il s'agit de nous dilater atome ou flûte de verre. Chute libre vers le pré.

## from L'Amer

À me morfondre sur un corps, à expier tous les symboles un à un, la violence, comme sur le bûcher les sorcières, une à une. Pour en finir avec l'expiation. La torture intérieure. La folie. C'est entre femmes que nous pourrons liquider la folie, sa fiction qu'elle me fascine, ce pouvoir de m'exciter moi de même qu'avec une autre femme, il faut, ce liquide dans ma moelle épinière, une identité.

Comme une grande trace de lèvres tenaces sur le clitoris, ça bouge, cet orgasme historique, celui de la rencontre des forces. L'excitation par la violence. Fantasme du sexe *opposé*. L'espèce, de corps meurtris.

longtemps longer nos corps encore à deux, à la faveur de la nuit. Folles et incompatibles comme deux hétérosexuelles avortées et qui ne peuvent se pénétrer mutuellement. La cicatrice doit cicatriser. Je mets ma bouche avec ton sexe. Salive intérieure. Manger et penser à notre fin.

NICOLE BROSSARD

# The Act of the Eye on Purple

*Some lesbian lovers have seen their eye become the eye of their lover in the distance.* MONIQUE WITTIG, SANDE ZEIG

As if to broach the vertigo, the smooth version of the shoulders of loving women's bodies or to find oneself there at the vital risk of lucidity women enlaced wonderful and close like a music. This evening, I run over and over in my head the foam and my mouth so that both shared in nourishing the meaning we find there stronger than the wind the sensation of bees, exhorting us into a garden. Slowly it entered through the eye, a serum, vital from one to the other. Women perturbed, new contingency, in a cycle to break through matters only when it is a question of our dilating atom or tulip glass. Free fall toward the meadow.

# from These Our Mothers

To work myself into the grave over a body, to expiate all the symbols one by one, violence, like the stake, the witches, one by one. To have done with expiation. Inner torture. Madness. Among women we could liquidate madness, its fiction how it fascinates me, this power to excite me just like with another woman, there must be, this liquid in my spinal cord, an identity.

Like a large mark of tenacious lips on the clitoris, it moves, this historical orgasm, this one about the meeting of forces. Excitation through violence. Phantasm of the oppos-ite sex. The species, from murdered bodies.

a long time lo(u)nging our bodies two-gether to pass under cover of night. Mad and incompatible like two aborted heterosexuals who cannot penetrate each other. The scar must form. I put my mouth with your sex. Inner saliva. Eat and think as though there were no end.

*Translated by* BARBARA GODARD

## The Silver Hook

Shower water tumbling down
her belly and into his mouth
(whose proverb? – that a fish
begins rotting from the head).
they spend the afternoon in bed,
four pillows of goose down, fresh
fruit from the coast, cold white
Ashkelon wine. she has painted
her toe-nails red. he smears
pulp and seed of berries over
her breasts. she licks his hands
clean, puts on a Bedouin skirt
that has jet glass eyes sewn
in the hem. in the shuttered light,
hair swept back, her throat
taut as a rope, she dances, arms
overhead and crossed at the wrists.
his shadow is thrown against the wall.
in the full-length mirror
the silver has shredded away
into a hole the shape of a hook.

## "Through Time and Bitter Distance"

Unknown to you, I walk the cheerless shore.
    The cutting blast, the hurl of biting brine
May freeze, and still, and bind the waves at war,
    Ere you will ever know, O! Heart of mine,
That I have sought, reflected in the blue
    Of these sea depths, some shadow of your eyes;
Have hoped the laughing waves would sing of you,
    But this is all my starving sight decries –

I

Far out at sea a sail
    Bends to the freshening breeze,
Yields to the rising gale
    That sweeps the seas;

II

Yields, as a bird wind-tossed,
    To saltish waves that fling
Their spray, whose rime and frost
    Like crystals cling

III

To canvas, mast and spar,
    Till, gleaming like a gem,
She sinks beyond the far
    Horizon's hem.

IV

Lost to my longing sight,
    And nothing left to me
Save an oncoming night, –
    An empty sea.

## Suzanne Takes You Down

Suzanne takes you down
to her place near the river,
you can hear the boats go by
you can stay the night beside her.
And you know that she's half crazy
but that's why you want to be there
and she feeds you tea and oranges
that come all the way from China.
Just when you mean to tell her
that you have no gifts to give her,
she gets you on her wave-length
and she lets the river answer
that you've always been her lover.
    And you want to travel with her,
    you want to travel blind
    and you know that she can trust you
    because you've touched her perfect body
    with your mind.

Jesus was a sailor
when he walked upon the water
and he spent a long time watching
from a lonely wooden tower
and when he knew for certain
only drowning men could see him
he said All men will be sailors then
until the sea shall free them,
but he himself was broken
long before the sky would open,
forsaken, almost human,
he sank beneath your wisdom like a stone.
    And you want to travel with him,

    you want to travel blind
    and you think maybe you'll trust him
    because he touched your perfect body
    with his mind.

Suzanne takes your hand
and she leads you to the river,
she is wearing rags and feathers
from Salvation Army counters.
The sun pours down like honey
on our lady of the harbour
as she shows you where to look
among the garbage and the flowers,
there are heroes in the seaweed
there are children in the morning,
they are leaning out for love
they will lean that way forever
while Suzanne she holds the mirror.
     And you want to travel with her
     and you want to travel blind
     and you're sure that she can find you
     because she's touched her perfect body
     with her mind.

## Metamorphose des amants

De partout la nuit craque et se fend
Et les amants se retrouvent couverts de plume
Avec un peu de sable sur les doigts.

Les amants ont soif dans leur lit desséché
Car toute l'eau est partie se noyer dans la mer;
Et les coqs à la fenêtre se poussent du jabot
Picorant dans la vitre les dernières étoiles.

Amants qui portez des panaches blancs et des couteaux
Saignez ces coqs et dans un plat de faïence
Répandez leur sang: qu'ils dorment, qu'ils dorment
Dans le cercle de craie où vos bras les ont clos.

## The Metamorphosis of Lovers

On all sides the night cracks & splinters
And lovers find themselves covered in feathers
With grains of sand between the fingers.

Lovers are thirsty in their drained beds
For all the moisture has left for the sea
And in the window the roosters are pouting,
Pecking in the glass the last stars.

Lovers who carry white plumes & knives
Bleed these cocks & in an earthenware bowl
Spread the blood: that they may sleep,
Sleep in the chalk circle your arms seal.

*Translated by* JOHN MONTAGUE

# The Sphinx In Toronto

## La Marche à l'amour

Tu as les yeux pers des champs de rosées
tu as des yeux d'aventure et d'années-lumière
la douceur du fond des brises au mois de mai
pour les accompagnements de ma vie en friche
avec cette chaleur d'oiseau à ton corps craintif
moi qui suis charpente et beaucoup de fardoches
moi je fonce à vive allure et entêté d'avenir
la tête en bas comme un bison dans son destin
la blancheur des nénuphars s'élève jusqu'à ton cou
pour la conjuration de mes manitous maléfiques
moi qui ai des yeux où ciel et mer s'influencent
pour la réverbération de ta mort lointaine
avec cette tache errante de chevreuil que tu as

tu viendras toute ensoleillée d'existence
la bouche envahie par la fraîcheur des herbes
le corps mûri par les jardins oubliés
où tes seins sont devenus des envoûtements
tu te lèves, tu es l'aube dans mes bras
où tu changes comme les saisons
je te prendrai marcheur d'un pays d'haleine
à bout de misères et à bout de démesures
je veux te faire aimer la vie notre vie
t'aimer fou de racines à feuilles et grave
de jour en jour à travers nuits et gués
de moellons nos vertus silencieuses
je finirai bien par te rencontrer quelque part
contre tout ce qui me rend absent et douloureux
par le mince regard qui me reste au fond du froid
j'affirme ô mon amour que tu existes
je corrige notre vie

nous n'irons plus mourir de langueur mon amour
à des milles de distance dans nos rêves bourrasques
des filets de sang dans la soif craquelée de nos lèvres
les épaules baignées de vols de mouettes
non
j'irai te chercher nous vivrons sur la terre
la détresse n'est pas incurable qui fait de moi

une épave de dérision, un ballon d'indécence
un pitre aux larmes d'étincelles et de lésions profondes
frappe l'air et le feu de mes soifs
coule-moi dans tes mains de ciel de soie
la tête la première pour ne plus revenir
si ce n'est pour remonter debout à ton flanc
nouveau venu de l'amour du monde
constelle-moi de ton corps de voie lactée
même si j'ai fait de ma vie dans un plongeon
une sorte de marais, une espèce de rage noire
si je fus cabotin, concasseur de désespoir
j'ai quand même idée farouche
de t'aimer pour ta pureté
de t'aimer pour une tendresse que je n'ai pas connue

dans les giboulées d'étoiles de mon ciel
l'éclair s'épanouit dans ma chair
je passe les poings durs au vent
j'ai un cœur de mille chevaux-vapeur
j'ai un cœur comme la flamme d'une chandelle
toi tu as la tête d'abîme douce n'est-ce pas
la nuit de saule dans tes cheveux
un visage enneigé de hasards et de fruits
un regard entretenu de sources cachées
et mille chants d'insectes dans tes veines
et mille pluies de pétales dans tes caresses

tu es mon amour
ma clameur mon bramement
tu es mon amour ma ceinture fléchée d'univers
ma danse carrée des quatre coins d'horizon
le rouet des écheveaux de mon espoir
tu es ma réconciliation batailleuse
mon murmure de jours à mes cils d'abeille
mon eau bleue de fenêtre
dans les hauts vols de buildings
mon amour
de fontaines de haies de ronds-points de fleurs
tu es ma chance ouverte et mon encerclement
à cause de toi

mon courage est un sapin toujours vert
et j'ai du chiendent d'achigan plein l'âme
tu es belle de tout l'avenir épargné
d'une frêle beauté soleilleuse contre l'ombre
ouvre-moi tes bras que j'entre au port
et mon corps d'amoureux viendra rouler
sur les talus du Mont-Royal
orignal, quand tu brames orignal
coule-moi dans ta palinte osseuse
fais-moi passer tout cabré tout empanaché
dans ton appel et ta détermination
Montréal est grand comme un désordre universel
tu es assise quelque part avec l'ombre et ton cœur
ton regard vient luire sur le sommeil des colombes
fille dont le visage est ma route aux réverbères
quand je plonge dans les nuits de sources
si jamais je te rencontre fille
après les femmes de la soif glacée
je pleurerait te consolerai
de tes jours sans pluies et sans quenouilles
des hasards de l'amour dénoué
j'allumerai chez toi les phares de la douceur
nous nous reposerons dans la lumière
de toutes les mers en fleurs de manne
puis je jetterai dans ton corps le vent de mon sang
tu seras heureuse fille heureuse
d'être la femme que tu es dans mes bras
le monde entier sera changé en toi et moi

la marche à l'amour s'ébruite en un voilier
de pas voletant par les eaux blessées de nénuphars
mes absolus poings
ah violence de délices et d'aval
j'aime
        que j'aime
                que tu t'avances
ma ravie
frileuse aux pieds nus sur les frimas
par ce temps doucement entêté de perce-neige

sur ces grèves où l'été
pleuvent en longues flammèches les cris des pluviers
harmonica du monde lorsque tu passes et cèdes
ton corps tiède de pruche à mes bras pagayeurs
lorsque nous gisons fleurant la lumière incendiée
et qu'en tangage de moisson ourlée de brises
je me déploie sur ta fraîche chaleur de cigale
je roule en toi
tous les saguenays d'eau noire de ma vie
je fais naître en toi
les frénésies de frayères au fond du cœur d'outaouais
puis le cri de l'engoulevent vient s'abattre dans ta gorge
terre meuble de l'amour ton corps
se soulève en tiges pêle-mêle
je suis au centre du monde tel qu'il gronde en moi
avec la rumeur de mon âme dans tous les coins
je vais jusqu'au bout des comètes de mon sang
haletant
                    harcelé de néant
                                        et dynamité
de petites apocalypses
les deux mains dans les furies dans les féeries
ô mains
ô poings
comme des cogneurs de folles tendresses

mais que tu m'aimes et si tu m'aimes
s'exhalera le froid natal de mes poumons
le sang tournera ô grand cirque
je sais que tout amour
sera retourné comme un jardin détruit
qu'importe je serai toujours si je suis seul
cet homme de lisière à bramer ton nom
éperdument malheureux parmi les pluies de trèfles
mon amour ô ma plainte
de merle-chat dans la nuit buissonneuse
ô fou feu froid de la neige
beau sexe floral ô ma neige
mon amour d'éclairs lapidée
morte
dans le froid des plus lointaines flammes

puis les années m'emportent sens dessus dessous
je m'en vais en délabre au bout de mon rouleau
des voix murmurent les récits de ton domaine
à part moi je me parle
que vais-je devenir dans ma force fracassée
ma force noire du bout de mes montagnes
pour te voir à jamais je déporte mon regard
je me tiens aux écoutes des sirènes
dans la longue nuit effilée du clocher de Saint-Jacques
et parmi ces bouts de temps qui halètent
me voici de nouveau campé dans ta légende
tes grands yeux qui voient beaucoup de cortège
les chevaux de bois de tes rires
tes yeux de paille et d'or
seront toujours au fond de mon cœur
et ils traverseront les siècles

## La Marche à l'amour

You have the blue-green eyes of fields in dew
adventurous eyes in which the light-years shine
you have the soft airs of winds in May
that birdlike from your timorous body play
an accompaniment through my uncleared fields
I who am timber and heaped brush
I who am drunk with the future, rush
headlong like a buffalo into his fate
the white of waterlilies rises to your throat
to conjure the dark manitous rising in my pulse
I in whose eyes the sea and sky conspire
for the reverberations of your far off death
in the telltale mark of the roe deer, your errant flesh

all sunlit with existence you will come
your mouth besieged by all the freshness of the grass
your body ripened in forgotten gardens
flowering in the incantations of your breasts
you rise, you are the morning breaking in my arms
to grow and change there as the seasons change
brave walker in a land of breath
I will take you to the end of this distress
I will take you to the end of all excess
I want to make you fall in love with life, our life
to love you madly, root and branch, and gravely
day by day, across the nights and across
the stony fords of our mute righteousness
I will meet you in the end, somewhere, someplace
in spite of everything that makes me absent, ache
with the meagre vision that is left me in the depths of cold
I affirm o my love that you exist
I correct our life

no more will we die of listlessness my love
before the endless miles in the squalls of our dreams
nor in the nets of blood, thirst's crackling on our lips
our shoulders bathed in flights of gulls
no
I will set out to find you, we will live on the earth

these straits that have reduced me to a drifting hulk
a balloon to be obscenely pricked, a clown
with starry tears and deeper wounds, are not invincible
beat up the air, beat up the fire of my desires
run me through the silken skies of your hands
headfirst, preventing my return
except I mount again becoming upright at your side
the newcomer sprung from the love of the world
constellate me in your body's milky way
even if I've made of my life's plunge
a sort of swamp, a kind of black rage
have been a wandering ham, gravel-crusher of despair
even so I am ferociously inclined
to love you still, to love you for your purity
and for a tenderness that I have never known

In sudden showers, stars bursting from my sky
the lightning streams through my flesh
and I go on fists clenched in the wind
a thousand horsepower beating in my heart
and in my heart a candle's flame
and you, your head holds all the mystery of a sweet abyss
is that not so
your hair the night of willow trees
your face is dusted with the snows
and fruits of fortune, and your gaze
is held still mistress to the hidden springs
and in your veins a thousand insects sing
and in your manifold caress a thousand petals rain

you are my love
my clamouring hooves, my bellowing
you are my love, my winter sash, orbiting the air
you are my square dance at the four corners of the world
my hank of hope, my spinning wheel
you are my deal
my fighting resolution to be reconciled
you are the hum of days before my grilled bee's eyes
my window of blue water in the high

flights of buildings, cries my love
of fountains, hedges, traffic circles filled with flowers
you are my chance in life, my prison yard
because of you
my courage is a spruce, forever green
my spirit's backboned with the rock bass
for you are beautiful
with all the spendings of the days to come
investing with frail sunlight all the poverty of dark
open your arms that I may enter port
my lover's body roll upon the talus of Mount Royal
my bellowing an echo to your bell
inhale me through your bony throat
and make me rear, parade in the panache
of your appeal and your determination
Montreal is large as all the world's disorder
somewhere in its shadows you are sitting and your heart
your gaze lights up the sleep of doves
girl whose face is now my lamplit route
as in the depths I plunge into the midnight springs
if ever I encounter you my girl
after all these women with their icy thirst
I will console you with my tears
for the days without rain or rushes green or thread to spin
for the risks of love once it's unwound
and I will light for you great lamps of tenderness
and we shall rest
in the light of the seas flowering in manna
then will I unleash
within your body all the winds of my blood
you will rejoice my girl you will rejoice
to be the woman that you are in my arms
the world in us will be transformed

the advance towards love now spreads to sail
with quivering stride on the waters wounded with lilies
my absolute fists
oh the violence of downstream, whirling delight
I love
      how I love
           how you advance
my ecstasy
shivering barefoot in the glittering frosts
in this season sweetly studded with snowdrops
on these shores where summer rains down
in long flakes the fiery cries of the plover
harmonica of the world as you pass and yield
your body warm as the birch bark in my paddler's arms
as we lie still, scenting the air in the burning light
as in the pitching harvest woven by the gales
I unfold in your warmth to the long cry of the cicada
in you I roll
my Saguenays, all the black waters of my life
in you I beget
the frenzies of the spawning grounds in the heart of the Ottawa
the cry of the nighthawk comes to beat in your throat
the earth, love's furniture, your flesh
erupts pell mell in fresh shoots
I am the center of the world as it groans
from the four corners of the globe with the rumour of my soul
I go to the very end of all the comets of my blood
panting
      harassed by the void
              dynamited
by a chronic small apocalypse
both hands in the fury of the storm, in fairyland
o hands
o fists
like hammers of a mad caress

because you love me and if you love me
the frost that was born in my lungs will breathe away
my blood revolve o magnificent circus
I know that love
will always be returned like a garden destroyed
what does it matter if I am alone I will always
be this marginal man belling your name
madly unhappy amid showers of sweet clover
my love o my complaint
of the catbird crying in the bushy night
sweet fool sweet fire sweet cold of the snow
my love defamed by the lightning stoned
dead
in the cold of the most distant flames

so willy nilly I am driven by the years
and I go on, run ragged, to the end of my rope
voices around me rumour your estate
and I say to myself
what's to become of me in my broken strength
my dark strength draining from my mountain base
to see you always I avert my sight
I stand alert for sirens in the long night
unwinding from the bell tower of St James
and in these whereabouts of time that pant
here I am again, my camp pitched amid your legend
your wide eyes that look out on so many processions
the painted horses of your laughter
your straw-flecked eyes, your gold eyes –
they will always be there in the bottom of my heart
they will travel through centuries by that art

*Translated by* D.G. JONES

LUDWIG ZELLER

# Memory's Vices

# The Brontë Sisters' Locket

DAVID MCFADDEN

## My Body Was Eaten by Dogs

I met her while walking in Egypt
on the road to Oxyrhynchus
where the Ibycus papyrus was found.
Her body had been eaten by dogs,
torn into little pieces,
each piece
            still glowing with life.

How I met her, I tripped on the road
then noticed the rock that caught my toe
was a face,
            a large broken nose and a
            once-smooth chin cracked and chipped.

She looked up at me with hardened eyes
silently pleading to be picked up

and I wondered what it would be like
to spend centuries without a workable body,
life clinging to small fragments of petrified flesh
like reflections to pieces of shattered glass

And there she was lying like a rock
in the road, helpless, a living
rock among all the other rocks,
a living planet searching the heavens
for signs of life.

And finally as I hesitated wondering
if I had time to waste on this, this . . .
I mean it was a curious situation all right
but the landscape was loaded, overloaded
with equally curious situations
and I was in a hurry to reach the sea

and the strange black mouth opened
and I had a glimpse of the awful warmth

of a life that has nothing else
but warmth.

*My body*, she said,
*was eaten by dogs.*

And her mouth slowly closed again
like a clam with a morsel to digest
and she continued staring up at me
as if I were the first person
in five thousand years
to have noticed her lying on the road

and I picked her up
and put her in my bag
and eventually brought her back to Canada

and now she is sitting on my bookshelf
in my home in Hamilton Ontario
and every nine minutes or so
she opens her mouth to say
*My body was eaten by dogs*

and her shrunken, blue-grey eyes
never close.

## The Death Agony of the Butterfly

a monarch beat its velvet brain
against the light, against
the cold light, I
thought of you.

*dance you, dance*
*you bitch*
*against the light against*
*the cold light,* that's
what you said.

always behind me, always
behind me is
your violent music, beat
until the butterfly's velvet brain
is dead.

*dance you, dance*
*you bitch, I*
*love you against*
*the light against*
*the cold light,* always
behind me is
your violent music.

## Doll House With Damp Walls: 10

I jacked her up with my bicycle pump:
(. . . the cross sweated, blood poured
from the flesh of a horse)
She rose straight up in the air
and came down in a men's room in Scranton.
The floor was a rainbow of tin,
held down by leather belts (I prefer
to keep my eyes open – let the salt run in).
Love came creeping
like a jack-knife at half-mast: Fatgut
American, carrying his head in a camera case (is this
what it will be like when haunted birds
lap the frozen air?); she heard
the dead end dial tone, exuberant
in its dark tower.
He gave her social reasons,
wrote letters, drove her to funerals,
watched for the black ice pellet in the water
and ravaged her; he was big:
she loved it, and drank a bottle of gin
to get rid of nothing. They ate each other
for 12 weeks. The wind froze in her body
and left all the kites and sun
drifting like a paper star (blood dried
on the flesh of the horse). So you see,
there have been no shadows in my life.
My loves are simple. Her legs were bare,
and wide, and in the morning
I sold my bicycle.

# Mai la nuit: 16

les draps froissés de chacun de tes cris
de tes cris les plus retenus
d'où s'échappe à peine un gémissement si bref
qu'il attaque dans leurs fondements les chambres

l'arc de tes cris au flanc de la main
tu dessines sur l'espace des oiseaux
des chevauchées
en élaguant la peur de ses divagations
les paupières brouillées parmi les cataractes
de sang
d'où nulle rivière ne coule plus
vers l'hypothétique océan
chevauchant côte à côte
les crinières dénouées
les crinières électriques
les fesses tannées au cuir des montures
dans le grand l'inexorable ralentissement
du mouvement

## May Night: 16

sheets rumpled by your cries
especially your muffled cries
letting only a little groan steal out
so brief
it saps rooms at their roots

your cries arc at the hand's flank
you sketch birds on space
cavaliers
pruning fear of frenzies
eyelids blurred among cataracts
of blood
from which no river flows
towards the alleged ocean
spuring side-by-side
flowing manes
electric manes
tanned haunches on the horses' hides
in the great unrelenting easing up
of movement

*Translated by* JOSÉE MICHAUD

## The Sleeping Lady XXXIII

I shall importune the blind white ghost . . .
fill her bowl with milk dreamier than snow.
– snakes love milk in lieu of lachrymose –
& I am cleansed by her alabescent glow.

Recumbent on a limb in my terrarium
Nadine lunched on a golden toad leaping air
excepting One who unzippered a gyrating rhythm:
– whose webbed fingers dimmed his own flame in despair –

Dressed in scintillating moonlight
she shimmered after straddlers out of lust
& flowing in a stream her eyes bloomed night
closing their silver on an eel in dust.

Temptress Nadine, some ice-worm'll visit you this Winter –
our reflection's shattered in every shard, & splinter.

## A Pastoral
*Adapted from Cavalcanti's*
BALLATA IX
"IN UN BOSCHETTO TROVAI PASTORELLA"


I wandered in a little wood, and there
I met a shepherdess. So fair
She seemed, I dreamed
She were a moonbeam, a fountain, or a star.

Her crispéd hair was gold.
Her eyes were made to hold
All love, in virtue far above
What may be told.

Her cheeks were white and red,
And with a wand her sheep she led.
The cold dew wet her pretty twinkling feet.
O love O love O love, she said.

Heart-touched, I did reply,
And gently asked her why
She walked alone, and made her plaintive moan
To stocks and stones, green trees, and the blue sky.

Softly she said, Alas
I have no man to pass
The time of the sweet spring with, or bring
Me solace.

When I hear the small bird sing
And see the flutter of his speckled wing
My heart turns over. I long for a lover
In the green wood in early spring.

When I heard this, and heard
The piping of the speckled bird
I said within my heart, Now bear a proper part,
And with a courteous word

I begged of her the grace
That I might kiss her face
And be the one alone,
Of her gentleness, in her embrace.

She took my hand and with a kindly will
Showed me a little hill
Wherein a stream did flow and flowers grow
And where (she said) the god of Love did dwell.

She was no moonbeam, star, or dream,
Nor icy changing crystal stream,
But very woman, such (I say) as no man
Might not love, nor her misdeem.

## Canadian Love Song

Your body's a small word with many meanings.
Love. If. Yes. But. Death.
Surely I will love you a little while,
perhaps as long as I have breath.

December is thirteen months long.
July's one afternoon; therefore
lovers must outwit wool,
learn how to puncture fur.

To my love's bed, to keep her warm,
I'll carry wrapped and heated stones.
That which is comfort to the flesh
is sometimes torture to the bones.

## Vers l'aube

Mon corps te parle te prend
en s'enfonçant dans le temps de ta chair.

Si usé si exsangue est ton songe,
si lépreuse mon agonie interminable
de bête errante.

Car je n'en finis plus de mourir
en rongeant le beau jade en ton âme.

Plus tu te donnes
plus je transhume d'éclair en éclair,
mais les vides me terrassent.

Que je suis en effroi quand j'entends l'aube
qui rôde qui m'attire qui me veut autre.

Mais je m'empierre l'oreille.

Je n'en finis plus de vouloir mourir.

## Towards Dawn

My body speaks to you takes you
burying itself in the moments of your flesh.
So worn so bloodless is your dream
so leprous my infinite agony
of the exhausted beast.

For I never stop dying
preying on the beautiful jade in your soul.

The more you give yourself
the more I graze my flocks on peak after peak
but the valleys drag me down.

How terrified I am when I hear the dawn
that prowls and attracts me wanting me changed.

But I block my ears.

I never stop wanting to die.

*Translated by* F.R. SCOTT

MARILYN BOWERING

## Well, it ain't no sin to take off your skin
## and dance around in your bones

I heard bones clacking last night
in the bed.
It was dreams, and not sleeping –
could it be a cold future?
There was snow on the morning ground.

I could hear skin, loose and naked
as it sloughed, layer by layer:

I liked its shape and hair and the pads
of its fingers,

but I could dance, I could dance with the bones.

Little lamb on the hillside,
you were drowning in snow,
and your ewe and shepherd danced over a stone:
warm rivers ran from those dancing feet
(black hooves and toes).

I slept badly last night,
listening to bones move like ancient wheels
over a slippery road.
They made a sound, chattering
like pebbles dropping down a mountain,

like hot streams bubbling from lava,
like a long time ago,

when there was you dancing, and me dancing.

## Chanson

J'ai fait mon ciel d'un nuage
Et ma forêt d'un roseau.
J'ai fait mon plus long voyage
Sur une herbe d'un ruisseau.

D'un peu de ciment : la ville
D'une flaque d'eau : la mer.
D'un caillou, j'ai fait mon île
D'un glaçon, j'ai fait l'hiver.

Et chacun de vos silences
Est un adieu sans retour,
Un moment d'indifférence
Toute une peine d'amour.

C'est ainsi que lorsque j'ose
Offrir à votre beauté
Une rose, en cette rose
Sont tous les jardins d'été.

# Song

I have made my sky from a cloud
And my forest from a reed.
I have made my longest journey
On a blade of grass in a stream.

From a little plaster, the city;
From a puddle of water, the sea.
From a pebble I made my island
And from an icicle, winter.

Each one of your silences
Is a parting without return
And a moment of indifference
The whole sorrow of love.

Thus it is when I dare
Offer your beauty
A rose, in this rose
Are all the gardens of summer.

*Translated by* A.J.M. SMITH

## HEAt MAkes TH HEARt's wINDOw

Onyx, th figure of her gaze
carries thruout long fields of snow
blowing, orange, th nails touching
        our wish clothd

    what metal holds, as th golden ring

raven, her hair, longer than ever is green
th sweet suckling tastes, meat to my brain
reaches, as th rainbow grows to circul
in th water pitcher

                    refreshes th thirst of
my memory, her limbs thrust
her fingers flying to my stroke

Under th mattress, a field of snow crystal
dry as th sun's heat
makes th rainbow glow

## Volets ouverts

j'habiterais cette musique un instant
comme un enfant lècherais la vitrine
d'où le soleil mène ses jardins à paître
et la nuit ses jardins à dormir
                              en passant

je traverserais la saison le fruit
la sentinelle heureuse et le pain
à peine ou entendrait mes pas
dans l'ardente prairie de ton rire
frémire étoiles sur ton sommeil

je retournerais sans mémoire
aux ventres noirs des fontaines
où la nuit dort au sein du jour
et dieu le serais bien malgré moi

dans le milieu de ton été

        l'étoile anneau douce à ton doigt
        j'y vois tourner la saison la ville la saison
        le temps abaisse sa paupière sur ton œil
        et le cœur violet de la fleur rougit ta chair
embrase ta lèvre
        où je bois le monde blessé guéri

        je t'aime et la terre à tes pieds se tait
comme la brebis mère endormie
        je t'aime et le ciel réfléchit ses miroirs
en ton sourire nuageux
        vienne la pluie        et ton corps soleil à travers
la pluie
        le monde est une fleur qui palpite à tes seins

choses qui naissent au sentier de tes doigts
jamais n'en referai le dessin sinon
qu'en la splendeur des lampes conjuguées
sur ton sommeil sous mon baiser

à l'orée de mes mains le clair de ton visage
chasseur à la trace des nuits je blêmissais
à renouer sur nos lèvres l'anneau de nos saisons

## Open Shutters

I would live for a moment in this music
like a child I would lick the windowpane
whence the sun leads his gardens out to pasture
and the night her gardens into sleep

                              on the way
I would pass through the season the fruit
the lucky sentinel and the bread
my steps barely heard
in the burning meadow of your laughter
like stars quivering above your sleep

I would return without memory
to the black bellies of the fountains
where night sleeps in the womb of day
and would be a god against my will

in the climate of your summer

in the ring-star soft on your finger
I see the season   the city   the season turning
time lowering its eyelids over your eye
and the flower's violet heart reddening your flesh
   setting your mouth ablaze
where I drink the wounded healed world

I love you and the earth is silent at your feet like
   a ewe asleep
I love you and the sky reflects its mirrors in your
   cloudy smile
comes the rain   and your body a sun through the
   rain
the world a flower which quivers at your breasts

the things which are born in the pathway of your
   fingers

never will I remake their design
save in the splendour of the lamps paired
above your sleep beneath my kiss

my cupped hands framing the light of your face
I a hunter on the trail of the nights turned pale
reforging on our lips the ring of our seasons

*Translated by* JOHN GLASSCO

## 'The Bellies of Fallen Breathing Sparrows'

Some things can't be praised enough, among them
breasts and birds
who have cohabited so long in metaphor
most folks think of them as married.
Not only that, but
when you slide your shirt (the striped one) off
the inside of my head is lined with down
like a Blackburnian warbler's nest,
the exterior of which is often rough and twiggy
in appearance.
And as the shirt snags, hesitates, and then
lets go, I know exactly why he warbles as he does,
which is zip zip zip zip zeee
        chickety chickety chickety chick.
The man who wrote "twin alabaster mounds"
should have spent more time outdoors
instead of browsing in that musty old museum where
he pissed away his youth.

## Arctic Rhododendrons

They are small purple surprises
in the river's white racket
and after you've seen them
a number of times
in water-places
where their silence seems
related to river-thunder
you think of them as 'noisy flowers'
Years ago
it may have been
that lovers came this way
stopped in the outdoor hotel
to watch the water floorshow
and lying prone together
where the purged green
boils to a white heart
and the shore trembles
like a stone song
with bodies touching
flowers were their conversation
and love the sound of a colour
that lasts two weeks in August
and then dies
except for the three or four
I pressed in a letter
and sent whispering to you

## Inside the Tulip

Inside the tulip
we make love
on closer look
seeing faint green lines, new

Let me share this flower
with you, kiss you
press my tongue on pollen
against the roof of my mouth

Look at me long enough
and I will be a flower
or wet blackberries dangling
from a dripping bush

Let me share you
with this flower, look
at anything long enough
and it is water

on a leaf, a petal
where we lie, bare legs together

## Seeds and Stars

when touch is merest wish we swim
like fish, our seed the liquid night,
the length of seas, our first deep element
and love is the end of sleep and sight

when wish is merest touch I bend
like her whose curve is heaven over earth
and love beneath me far and far
makes my flesh a miracle of stars

## Balloon Flowers

In the greenhouse
I'm staring down at pregnancies; tiny zeppelins –
skins: leopard
    clotted
        – soul's orgasm – bal
         loon flowers

              I reach out to touch
              I tickle their ear lobes
              rub the triggers
              of each
                      balloon flower, they
                      don't complain, but
                      blush out
                      at my fingers, o
                      what distilled
                      manures & minerals
                      nourished
                      these
                      air
                      brothels.
                      I'm staring at bellies
                      clotted with leopard:
                      zeppelins swelling out
                      happy
                      pregnancies. ALIEN
                        GLANDS,
                      they are not of this planet
                      these pregnancies: I touch
                      touch
                      fungus dreams, touch
                      passions of leopard
                      painted
                      on
                      blood
                      blood

                      blood

# Romantic Prairie Life

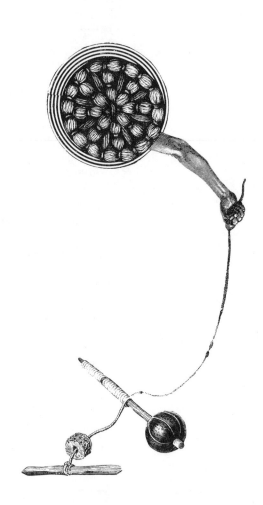

MILTON ACORN: "Invocation." Published in *Dig Up My Heart: Selected Poems 1952–83* (Toronto: McClelland and Stewart Limited, 1983). Reprinted by permission of the author.

MARGARET ATWOOD: "Variation On The Word Sleep." Published in *True Stories* (Toronto: Oxford University Press, 1981). Reprinted by permission of the author.

MARGARET AVISON: "Water and Worship: An open-air service on the Gatineau River." Published in *Sunblue* (Hantsport: Lancelot Press, 1978). Reprinted by permission of the publisher. "Person, or A Hymn on and to the Holy Ghost." Published in *Winter Sun / The Dumbfounding* (Toronto: McClelland and Stewart Limited, 1981). Used by permission of The Canadian Publishers, McClelland and Stewart Limited, Toronto.

MICHEL BEAULIEU: "Mai la nuit: 16." Published in *Visages* (Montréal, Éditions du Noroît, 1981). Reprinted by permission of the author.

EARLE BIRNEY: "I should have begun with your toes." Published in *Fall By Fury* (Toronto: McClelland and Stewart Limited, 1978). "Wind Chimes," "There Are Delicacies." Published in *Ghost In The Wheels* (Toronto: McClelland and Stewart Limited, 1977). Used by permission of The Canadian Publishers, McClelland and Stewart Limited, Toronto.

BILL BISSETT: "HEAt MAkes TH HEARt's wINDOw." Published in *Beyond Even Faithful Legends* (Vancouver: Talonbooks, 1980). Reprinted by permission of the author.

ROO BORSON: "Gray Glove." Published in *A Sad Device* (Montréal: Quadrant Editions, 1981). Reprinted by permission of the author.

GEORGE BOWERING: "Inside The Tulip." Published in *The Silver Wire* (Kingston: Quarry Press, 1966). Reprinted by permission of the author.

MARILYN BOWERING: "It aint no sin to take off your skin and dance around in your bones." Published in *Giving Back Diamonds* (Victoria: Press Porcépic, 1982). Reprinted by permission of the author.

JACQUES BRAULT: "Connaissance." Published in *Mémoire* (Paris: Grasset, 1968). Reprinted by permission of the author.

ROBERT BRINGHURST: "These Poems, She Said." Published in *The Beauty Of The Weapons* (Toronto: McClelland and Stewart Limited,

1981). Used by permission of The Canadian Publishers, McClelland and Stewart Limited, Toronto.

NICOLE BROSSARD: "L'amèr: ou le Chapitre effrité." Published in *L'Amèr: ou le Chapitre effrité* (Montréal: Les Editions Quinze, 1977). Reprinted by permission of the publisher.

BARRY CALLAGHAN: "Fire And Water." Published in *As Close As We Came* (Toronto: Exile Editions Ltd., 1982). "The Gift of Tongue," "The Silver Hook." Published in *The Hogg Poems And Drawings* (Toronto: General Publishing, 1978). Reprinted by permission of the author.

PAUL CHAMBERLAND: "Volets Ouverts." Published in *Terre Québec* (Montréal: Déom, 1964). Reprinted by permission of the author.

LEONARD COHEN: "For Anne," "As The Mist Leaves No Scar," "Now Of Sleeping." Published in *The Spice-Box of Earth* by Leonard Cohen Copyright © Leonard Cohen. Used by permission. All rights reserved. "Suzanne." Published in *Parasites Of Heaven* by Leonard Cohen. Copyright © Leonard Cohen. Used by permission. All rights reserved. "Slowly I Married Her." Published in *Death Of A Lady's Man* by Leonard Cohen. © Leonard Cohen. Used by permission. All rights reserved.

JOHN ROBERT COLOMBO: "123456789K.O." PUBLISHED IN *How Do I Love Thee* (Edmonton: M.G. Hurtig, 1970). Reprinted by permission of the translator.

DAVID DONNELL: "Walking." Published in *Dangerous Crossings* (Windsor, Black Moss Press, 1980). Reprinted by permission of the author.

RAOUL DUGUAY: "123456789K.O." PUBLISHED IN *L'Apokalipsô* (Montréal: Éditions du Jours, 1971). Reprinted by permission of the author.

RAY ELLENWOOD: "Megalomaniac Shields." Published in *Ellipse 17*, 1975. Reprinted by permission of the translator.

CLAUDE GAUVREAU: "Boucliers mégalomanes." Published in *Oeuvres Créatrices Complètes* (Montréal: Éditions Parti Pris, 1971). Reprinted by permission of the author's estate.

JOHN GLASSCO: "Open Shutters," "Et je prierai ta grâce." Published in *The Poetry of French Canada In Translation* (Toronto: Oxford University Press, 1970). Reprinted by permission of the author's estate.

BARBARA GODARD: "The Act Of The Eye On Purple," "These Our Mothers." Published in *These Our Mothers Or: The Disintegrating Chapter* (Toronto: Coach House Press, 1983). Reprinted by permission of the translator.

ALAIN GRANDBOIS: "L'Aube ensevelie." Published in *Poèmes* (Montréal: Éditions de l'Hexagone, 1963). Reprinted by permission of the publisher.

ANNE HÉBERT: "La Fille maigre," "Il y a certainement quelqu'un." Published in *Tombeau des Rois* (Paris: Éditions du Seuil, 1953). Reprinted by permission of the author.

D.G. JONES: "From Sex, This Sea." Published in *Under The Thunder The Flowers Light Up The Earth* (Toronto: Coach House Press, 1977). "The Virgin Burned." Published in *The Terror Of The Snows* (Pittsburgh: The University of Pittsburgh Press, 1976). "*La Marche à l'amour.*" Published in *Ellipse 5*, 1970. Reprinted by permission of the author and translator.

DIANE KEATING: "The Dead Sky Letters," "Fecundity." Published in *No Birds Or Flowers* (Toronto: Exile Editions, 1982). Reprinted by permission of the author.

ROBERT KROETSCH: "Pumpkin: A Love Poem." Published in *The Stone Hammer Poems* (Nanaimo: Oolichan Books, 1975). Reprinted by permission of the author.

PAUL-MARIE LAPOINTE: "Le Vierge incendié." Published in *Le Réel Absolu* (Montréal: Éditions de l'Hexagone, 1971). Reprinted by permission of the author.

PATRICK LANE: "Gray John," "Gray Silk Twisting." Published in *Beware The Months Of Fire* (Toronto: Anansi, 1974). Reprinted by permission of the author.

IRVING LAYTON: "An Old Niçoise Whore," "The Day Aviva Came To Paris," "Proteus And Nymph." Published in *A Wild Peculiar Joy: Selected Poems 1945–82* (Toronto: McClelland and Stewart Limited, 1982). Used by permission of The Canadian Publishers, McClelland and Stewart Limited, Toronto.

DOROTHY LIVESAY: "Bartok and the Geranium." Published in *Collected Poems; the two seasons* (Toronto: McGraw-Hill Ryerson Limited, 1972). Reprinted by permission of the publisher.

GWENDOLYN MACEWEN: "Seeds and Stars," "The Death Agony of the

Butterfly." Published in *Earth-light* (Toronto: General Publishing, 1982). "Arcanum One," "Arcanum Four," "Arcanum Seven." Published in *Magic Animals: Selected Poems Old And New* (Toronto: Macmillam of Canada Limited, 1974). Reprinted by permission of the author.

JAY MAC PHERSON: "Eurynome II," "Garden Of The Sexes." Published in *Poems Twice Told* (Toronto: Oxford University Press, 1981). Reprinted by permission of the author.

ROBERT MARTEAU: "Métamorphose des amants." Published in *Royaumes* (Paris: Éditions du Seuil, 1962). Reprinted by permission of the author.

STEVEN MC CAFFERY: "Carnival." Published in *Carnival: The First Panel: 1967–70* (Toronto: Coach House Press, 1973). Reprinted by permission of the author.

DAVID MC FADDEN: "My Body Was Eaten By Dogs." Published in *On The Road Again* (Toronto: McClelland and Stewart Limited, 1978). Used by permission of The Canadian Publishers, McClelland and Stewart Limited, Toronto.

DON MC KAY: " 'The Bellies of Fallen Breathing Sparrows.' " Published in *Birding, or Desire* (Toronto: McClelland and Stewart Limited, 1983). Used by permission of The Canadian Publishers, McClelland and Stewart Limited, Toronto.

JOSÉE MICHAUD: "May Night." Published in *Visages* (Toronto: Exile Editions, 1984). Reprinted by permission of the translator.

PETER MILLER: "The Shrouded Dawn." Published in *Selected Poems* (Toronto: Contact Press, 1964). Reprinted by permission of the translator.

GASTON MIRON: "La Marche à l'amour." Published in *l'Homme rapaillé* (Montréal: Les Presses de l'Université de Montréal, 1970). Reprinted by permission of the author.

JOHN MONTAGUE: "The Metamorphosis of Lovers." Published in *Exile*, *Vol. 1*, No. 2, 1973. Reprinted by permission of the translator.

SUSAN MUSGRAVE: "Coming Of Age." Published in *A Man To Marry A Man To Bury* (Toronto: McClelland and Stewart Limited, 1979). Used by permission of The Canadian Publishers, McClelland and Stewart Limited, Toronto.

JOHN NEWLOVE: "Lady, Lady." Published in *The Fat Man: Selected Poems 1962–1972* (Toronto: McClelland and Stewart Limited, 1977).

Used by permission of The Canadian Publishers, McClelland and Stewart Limited, Toronto.

ALDEN NOWLAN: "Canadian Love Song." Published in *Early Poems* (Fredericton: Fiddlehead, 1983). Reprinted by permission of the author's estate.

b. p. NICHOL: "Blues." Typography by Vivien Halas. Published in *Concrete Poetry: Britain, Canada, United States* (Stuttgart and London: Editions Hansjorg Mayer, 1967). Reprinted by permission of the author.

MICHAEL ONDAATJE: "White Room," "Moon Lines, After Jiménez." Published in *There's a Trick with a Knife I'm Learning to Do* (Toronto: McClelland and Stewart Limited, 1979). "The Cinnamon Peeler." Published in *Running In The Family* (Toronto: McClelland and Stewart Limited, 1983). Reprinted by permission of the author.

FERNAND OUELLETTE: "Communication," "Vers l'aube." Published in *Poésie* (Montréal, Éditions de l'Hexagone, 1972). Reprinted by permission of the author.

P. K. PAGE: "Water And Marble," "Personal Landscape." Published in *Poems Selected And New* (Toronto: Anansi, 1974). Reprinted by permission of the author.

AL PURDY: "Necropsy of Love." Published in *The Caribou Horses* (Toronto: McClelland and Stewart Limited, 1965). "Love At Roblin Lake." Published in *Being Alive: Poems 1958–78* (Toronto: McClelland and Stewart Limited, 1978). "Arctic Rhododendrons." Published in *North of Summer* (Toronto: McClelland and Stewart Limited, 1967). Used by permission of The Canadian Publishers, McClelland and Stewart Limited, Toronto.

JOE ROSENBLATT: "The Mushroom Factory," "Balloon Flowers," "It Was Never Like This Before," "Love Poem For Faye." Published in *Top Soil* (Erin: Press Porcépic Limited, 1976). "The Sleeping Lady XXXIII." Published in *The Sleeping Lady* (Toronto: Exile Editions Ltd., 1979). Reprinted by permission of the author.

WILLIAM RONALD: "Doll House With Damp Walls." Published in *Exile*, Vol. 2, No. 1, 1974. Reprinted by permission of the author.

SAINT-DENYS-GARNEAU: "Et je prierai ta grâce." Published in *Poésies complètes* (Montréal, Les Éditions Fides, 1972). Reprinted by permission of the author's estate.

ALLAN SAFARIK: "God Loves Us Like Earthworms Love Wood."

Published in *God Loves Us Like Earthworms Love Wood* (Erin: The Porcupine's Quill, 1983). Reprinted by permission of the author.

R. MURRAY SCHAFER: "/ ϽϪ/ Ͻ\Ξ" Published in / ϽϪ/ Ͻ\Ξ (Toronto: Exile Editions Ltd., 1977). Reprinted by permission of the author.

F.R. SCOTT: "The Lean Girl," "There Is Certainly Someone." Published in *Saint-Denys-Garneau & Anne Hébert* (Vancouver: Klanak Press, 1962). "Knowing." Published in *The Poetry of French Canada in Translation* (Toronto: Oxford University Press, 1970). "Communion," "Towards Dawn." Published in *Poems of French Canada* (Burnaby: Blackfish Press, 1977). Reprinted by permission of the author's estate.

LARRY SHOULDICE: "The Virgin Burned." Published in *Ellipse 11*, 1972. Reprinted by permission of the translator.

ROBIN SKELTON: "Wart Hog." Published in *Timelight* (Toronto: McClelland and Stewart Limited, 1974). Used by permission of The Canadian Publishers, McClelland and Stewart Limited, Toronto.

A. J. M. SMITH: "A Pastoral," "An Iliad For His Summer Sweetheart." Published in *The Classic Shade* (Toronto: McClelland and Stewart Limited, 1978). Reprinted by permission of the publisher. "Song." Published in *The Poetry of French Canada in Translation* (Toronto: Oxford University Press, 1970). Reprinted by permission of the translator's estate.

GILLES VIGNEAULT: "Chanson." Published in *Silences: poems 1957–77* (Montréal: Nouvelles Éditions d'ARC, 1978). Reprinted by permission of the author.

GEORGE YEMEC: "Flic." Published in *The River's Bend Review* (Toronto: 1973). Reprinted by permission of the author.

LUDWIG ZELLER: "Lovers." Published in *Alphacollage: An Alphabet of Twenty-Seven Letters* (Erin: The Porcupine's Quill, 1982). "The Sphinx in Toronto," "Romantic Prairie Life," "Memory's Vices," "The Brontë Sisters' Locket." Published in *50 Collages* (Oakville: Mosaic Press, 1981). Reprinted by permission of the author.

ROBERT ZEND: "Confession." Published in *Exile, Vol. 2*, No. 2, 1974. Reprinted by permission of the author.